Cultural Encounters

İnci Bilgin Tekin

Cultural Encounters

Intertextual and Intergeneric Dialogues

PETER LANG

Berlin · Bruxelles · Chennai · Lausanne · New York · Oxford

Bibliographic Information published by the Deutsche Nationalbibliothek
The Deutsche Nationalbibliothek lists this publication in the Deutsche Nationalbibliografie;
detailed bibliographic data is available online at http://dnb.d-nb.de.

Library of Congress Control Number: 2025926524

ISBN 978-3-631-94666-4 (Print)
ISBN 978-3-631-94667-1 (E-PDF)
ISBN 978-3-631-94668-8 (E-PUB)
DOI 10.3726/b23409

© 2025 Peter Lang Group AG, Lausanne (Switzerland)
Published by Peter Lang GmbH, Berlin (Germany)

info@peterlang.com

This publication has been peer reviewed.

www.peterlang.com

I wish to dedicate this study to the writing process itself.
To the canonised and noncanonised…

Acknowledgements

This book owes to my summer-long affiliation with the Shakespeare Library at Ludwig Maximilian University in München. I wish to express my gratitude to Prof. Claudia Olk for hosting my study in such a challenging research environment. My heartfelt thanks go to my lifelong academic mentor, Prof. Özden Sözalan, for being always so supportive and providing us with such a distinct atmosphere of study at İstanbul Bilgi University, Department of English Language and Literature, as head of the department. I owe a special thanks to Prof. Aslı Tekinay, whom I keep consulting at each and every academic step I take, ever since I took her inspiring drama lectures at Boğaziçi University. I feel indebted to my dear colleague and beloved friend, Prof. Naz Bulamur, for her invaluable support and constructive suggestions during this study. Many thanks to my postdoc academic sponsor, Prof. Deborah Cartmell, for enabling such secure access to the fantastic world of Adaptation Studies. I also wish to express my gratitude to my dear colleagues at İstanbul Bilgi University, Faculty of Social Sciences and Humanities, and my dear students at İstanbul Bilgi University and Boğaziçi University for the intriguing discussions feeding this study.

Another heartfelt thanks goes to dear members of my family for bearing with me at each and every stage of this journey. My lifelong partner, Dr. Bülent Tekin, my inspiring son, Mert Tekin, my creative daughter, Derin Tekin, my loving parents, Prof. Leman Bilgin and Servet Bilgin, my beloved sister, Güller Pınar Bilgin, without your enduring support, this would not have been possible. Each and every academic work reflects an accumulation of emotional and intellectual wealth. I feel grateful to my late grandparents,

Mustafa Sami-Yıldız Dinçer and Ahmet-Fatma Ayten Bilgin, for initiating my intellectual enthusiasm in reading and writing. Heartfelt thanks to all my teachers, lecturers and storytellers, established writers and potential ones as well as keen readers, whose indirect presence I can trace in each and every word I have been writing.

Contents

CONTENTS

Introduction

This book contextually, methodologically and structurally draws on inter-textual engagements, which are connected and responsive to one another, within a broadly given context of cultural encounters.

Both the texts that are dealt within the chapters and the chapters them-selves share a common ground in approaching intertextuality as a counter-oppressive method, accommodating postcolonial, feminist posthumanist and therefore intersectionally inclusive responses to the hegemonic discourses.

This study owes its inspiration to the everlasting process of literary dia-logue, which dates back to classical antiquity. Although its recognition as a point of reference can be traced to the rise of modernism, "intertextual" and "intergeneric" relations have become specific fields of research only after the 1960s, a noteworthy time period to announce not only the birth of the poststructuralist approach but also the rise of postcolonial and feminist movements. While simultaneously, reader-response theory urges a reposi-tioning of the writer and the reader within textuality by crediting readerly involvement, intertextuality and rewrite started to appear on the literary agenda. Translation and Adaptation Studies were inevitably fed by these new approaches, which reintroduce both the translator and the adaptor as the "rewriter" while the definition of rewrite involves extended and targeted inter-textual dialogue with a canonical text. With the flourishing of Adaptation Studies and the shifting trend in Translation Studies from a writer-centred approach to a target culture-centred approach in the late 1960s, adaptation and translation studies scholars have displayed an ever-growing interest in intertextual and intergeneric relations. However, their enthusiasm for the new form of dialogue has unfortunately blocked the postcolonial, feminist and/or posthumanistic discourses, running parallel to these movements' common motivation to extend intertextuality studies: subversion as a method for revolution. Having observed that the three counter-oppression-driven movements have hardly received the critical attention they deserve within Adaptation and Translation Studies, this study hopes to contribute to extended studies on intertextuality by addressing this field of study as a potentially strong ground for postcolonial, feminist and posthumanist agendas.

> Even in the simplest story there is bound to be some kind of blockage, if only for the fact that no can ever be told in its entirety. Indeed, it is only through inevitable omissions that a story will gain its dynamism. Thus whenever the flow is interrupted and we are led off in unexpected directions, the opportunity is given to bring into play our own faculty for establishing connections- for filling in the gaps left by the text itself (216).

The above-quoted lines by Wolfgang Iser address the ever continuous process of storytelling, highlighting the most significant function of the story-teller, namely to tell a tale with an individual focus. Iser's lines point out that, despite the individual engagement of the story-teller, stories belong to a collective axis, as issued by the cultural context of story-telling itself. Given this context, stories can be defined as individual reflections on collective experiences, through which the agent, as the story-teller, transcends over subjectivity and reaches a level of collectivity, where passing on this specific experience becomes more significant than the subjective gaze filtering it. Located within a surrounding cultural axis, it is no wonder that stories inevitably involve similar themes and/or patterns.

In his celebrated essay "Myth Today", Roland Barthes suggests that myths never die, but keep transforming (261, 262). Working on repetitive patterns embedded in myths, Levi Strauss' inspiring essay entitled "The Structural Study of Myth" puts forth the idea that the structural units within myths, "mythemes", are "fundamental" units functioning similarly within their group (428–432). These approaches also neglect the possibility of "originality" or "authenticity" in stories.

Story-telling can be traced back as early as 3000 BC, a time long before written language was introduced. In her comprehensive study on myths, Edith Hamilton notes that myths project the thoughts and feelings of the human race in told ages (13), highlighting mankind's long tradition of story-telling. Studies on myths demonstrate that stories as myths and legends go much beyond recognition of any form or structure. As Edith Hamilton puts it, myths reflect a time "when the world was still young" and mankind was located at the heart of nature (13–14), without any cultural recognition, until the first city-state structure. Mankind's earliest orientation to literary form is, indeed, through Aristotle's *Poetics* (fourth-century BC), which is the first text to set the standards for generic definitions. Aristotle's division of literary genres as "tragedy", "epic" and "comedy", in accordance with the hierarchical sequence he suggests for the study of genres, has still provided a noteworthy reference for contemporary literary scholarship.

The Industrial Revolution (1760), which inevitably introduced a new definition of culture through urbanisation, mass production and consumption, paved the way for man's experiment with new methods, weigh outside the axis of the mid-seventeenth century Neo-classical tradition, the mission of which is addressed below by the celebrated Augustan poet, Alexander Pope:

First follow Nature, and your judgement frame
By her just standard, which is still the same (Pope L 1, 2).

In their understanding, echoing nature as "methodized" is the ultimate path to undertake for a true communication with the classics (Pope L 3–8). In other words, departure from nature would ontologically problematise a work of art in its classical definition. The Romantic poet William Wordsworth points out the changing understanding of culture after the Industrial Revolution as if antagonist to nature:

The world is too much with us; late and soon,
Getting and spending, we lay waste our Powers,
Little we see in Nature that is ours;
We have given our hearts away, a sordid boon! (Wordsworth L, 1–4)

With the rise of Modernism, a nostalgic search for connection with the past becomes foregrounded and a revival of interest in the classics becomes inevitable. T. S. Eliot's celebrated essay *Tradition and the Individual Talent* (1919) highlights the modern writer's underlying process of "self sacrifice" by borrowing from and putting back to "tranquility" (1919: 1–7). T.S. Eliot's early twentieth-century work places the concept in a modernist context by drawing on a system of relations between the past and the present. "No poet, no artist of any art, has his complete meaning alone." His significance, his appreciation is the appreciation of his relation to the dead poets and artists. "What happens is a continual surrender of himself as he is at the moment to something which is more valuable. The progress of an artist is a continual self-sacrifice, a continual extinction of personality", which he calls "depersonalization" (1919: 3). T.S. Eliot has a noteworthy contribution to studies on intertextuality by pointing out both "tradition" and the new poet's "individual difference" (1919: 2) as well as addressing "the emotion of art" as "impersonal" and inevitably connected to the artist's relation to "his predecessors" (1919: 7).

In his work *The Anxiety of Influence: A Theory of Poetry* (1973), Harold Bloom offers a psychoanalytical reading of the new generation poet ("ephebe") in relation to the old generation poet ("predecessor") in the Freudian Oedipal triangle. This psychoanalytical study by Bloom is also noteworthy in introducing a different perspective to intertextual relations as well as authorial dialogues. Bloom's study provides an in-depth analysis of the subjective process the writer goes through as an individual. The contemporary writer's readerly admiration for the canonical writer and his anxiety that stems from the possibility of not going further than the canonical writer is viewed in allusion to the son's Oedipal relation with the father which builds on both "admiration" and "rivalry" (1973: 140–150).

Roland Barthes's celebrated study titled *The Rustle of Language* (1984) provides a new dimension to the understanding of textuality as it explores the text within a "multidimensional space" (53), consisting of a multiplicity of textualities. To put it in Barthes's own words:

> The text is a fabric of quotations, resulting from a thousand sources of culture. The writer can only imitate an ever anterior, never original gesture, his sole power is to mingle writings, to counter some by others and this book itself is but a tissue of quotations, infinitely postponed (1984: 53).

Barthes's understanding neglects the idea of originality in the writing process and defines the writing process within an act of "imitation" and "quotation". In his highly cited work, 'The Death of the Author' (1967), Barthes also owns a poststructuralist perspective toward the text and thereby invites the reader to undertake a dynamic role within the reading process and becomes a noteworthy reference point for reader response criticism. Questioning the authority of the writer over the text neglects the idea of a finished text, introducing room for the reader's dynamic involvement.

In other words, no text can ever be thought outside surrounding cultural contexts, a predicate to suggest that the notion of textuality inevitably entails arbitrary or intended dialogue. The feminist theorist Julia Kristeva coined the term "intertextuality" in her essay "Word, Dialogue and the Novel" (1966) published in her longer work titled *Desire in Language: A Semiotic Approach To Literature and Art* (1969), where she defines the concept in relation to "inter-subjectivity" and dialogue, as a "process", drawing on dynamism within the text itself (1969: 64–66). Drawing on Kristeva, intertextuality can be viewed as a reference to both readerly and writerly consciousnesses at once and in collaboration. In her invaluable study *Playing in the Dark*, Toni Morrison also acknowledges that "reading and writing are not that distinct for a writer" (1993: 22). This dynamic approach, which refuses to define the reader and writer within the limits of one specific text and prefers to relocate these concepts on a dynamic axis of textualities, favours collectivity and highlights collaboration in production despite the classical approach to the writer as the agent of production and the reader, that of consumption. The idea that readers can be potential writers of a prospective text and writers are also readers of previous texts points out that literary dialogues between past, present and future are inescapable and references to the canon are, therefore, inevitable. Given this context, any writing implies an interwoven process of rewriting and, in its broadest definition to involve the translator (Lefevere 3–5), the rewriter undertakes the role of a mediator between the readerly and writerly processes, which is a prerequisite for any intertextual engagement.

Although the term "intertextuality" was not coined before the rise of the poststructuralist wave in the 1960s, its history can be traced to classical literature when Seneca (first-century AD) offers his own versions of *Medea*, *Oedipus* and *Agamemnon*, plays associated with his predecessors Euripides, Sophocles and Aeschylus, respectively. Although it is usually identified with a satirical perspective, the first genre that accommodates adaptive qualities may be considered as classical parody, dating back to Aristotelian times. Parody is a style recurring in different times and traditions of literature, from Aristophanes of classical Greek to Geoffrey Chaucer of the Medieval English, from Cervantes of seventeenth-century Spain to Henry Fielding of eighteenth-century England. "Imitation" or "inspiration" can be noted among the most recurrent terms in early theoretical works by Plato, Horace and Longinus (first-century BC), the first person to directly theorise, being gradually shaped into our contemporary consciousness.

In her comprehensive work *A Theory of Parody*, Linda Hutcheon argues that postmodern parody, which accounts for the contemporary experience, replaces the satirical perspective of the classical parody by "repetition with a critical distance" (2001: 32). As Hutcheon acknowledges writing her later work *A Theory of Adaptations*, there is a close link between parody and adaptation. Ever since 1970s, when adaptation studies were first introduced as a new academic field building on interdisciplinary approaches, the major debate among the adaptation studies scholars has always been the issue of fidelity in adaptations. Parallel to both the post-1960s transformation of translation studies from a source-text oriented approach to a target-text oriented one, and the groundbreaking suggestion that reader-centred criticism should replace author-centred perspectives (late 1960s), adaptation studies have also developed the notion of "free" or "loose" adaptations, which are also called "appropriations".

Adaptation, by its lexical definition, is "to make suitable" to another context, which inevitably requires an intercultural or intergeneric transfer. Intertextuality, which draws on literary dialogue, is broader than the specific and central case of adaptation. To Linda Hutcheon, adaptation implies "an acknowledged transposition of a recognizable work in a process of creation and reception" (2006: 8), involving both "difference" and "repetition" (2006: 114). An earlier theorist, Geoffrey Wagner, classifies adaptation as "transposition, commentary and analogue" (1975: 20–21). In this respect, adaptation is a translational and analytical process that requires an intentional engagement with the source text, offering new interpretive contributions. In a broader sense, adaptation is the text meant for the target context and thus the outcome of any intercultural encounter, as accommodated by an intergeneric relationship. In his groundbreaking work titled "The Law of Genre", Jacques Derrida questions whether genres can be mixed, as he starts with an ironic predicate suggesting "genres are not to be mixed. I will not mix them" (web 203). With a sarcastic attitude embedded in his language, Derrida highlights that genres are normative. In other words, once genre is taken into consideration, it is inevitably treated as if a law, calling for the recognition of its "limits" in defining itself and its "other" (web 203–205). Derrida's inspiring approach to the ontology of genres has greatly contributed to the rising body of studies on intergeneric relations and reinforced the generic theories on adaptation studies.

Focusing on its dialogue with different "medium[s]", Imelda Whelehan views adaptation studies as a "hybrid" kind of study (2010, 3). Similarly, Julie Sanders builds on Homi K. Bhabha and considers adaptation as a "hybridized form" (2006, 17–19). Its "hybridity" owes to its translational status in-between not only two genres or two disciplines but also two different cultural contexts. Adaptation's broad intertextual engagement also involves a spatial or temporal transfer, which reinforces its in-between or "hybrid" status. Adaptation, a term to imply both the process and the product, is the outcome of an intercultural encounter in its broadest sense. To put its authentic position in Linda Hutcheon's words, "an adaptation has its own aura" (2006: 6). The idea of adapting implies an intergeneric encounter along with an intertextual one. Text-to-text, text-to-stage and text-to-screen adaptations commonly build on a journey in between different genres. In this respect, the "aura" of adaptation owes much to its innately in-between form.

Ever since Geoffrey Wagner's publication of *The Novel and The Cinema* in 1975, the question of "fidelity versus betrayal" to the source text has been the major point of departure for many adaptation studies scholars. Some suggest that the adapter should be careful while in such a dialogue with a canonical work, whereas others argue on the side of "free adaptations". As Linda Hutcheon puts it, "[a]daptation is repetition, but repetition without replication" (2006: 7), as well as "[…] a derivation that is not derivative -a work that is second without being secondary" (2006: 9). Drawing on Hutcheon's words, which do not undermine the "creative" and "interpretive" process in such "acknowledged transpositions" (8), adaptations can be viewed as innovative transformations. While the conventional method in adaptation studies is to look at omissions from and additions to the source text, recent theories tend to focus on the adaptation more than the source text itself. This recent trend also justifies its method by suggesting that a good adaptation also contributes to the reception of its source text by offering a new critical dimension to studies on the canonical work. In this respect, even the most free or loose adaptations or "appropriations" function not across but towards the canonical source text.

Owing to the innovative perspective as well as the transformative structure they offer, adaptations frequently accommodate strong discourses and especially invite counter-oppression-driven ideologies such as postcolonial and feminist criticism. Surrounded by both the thematic and structural power of transformation, adaptation also signifies resistance to old understandings and forms. The closer the product gets into being an appropriation, the more subversive the process becomes. Appropriations are free adaptations involving more secondary relation with more indirect reference to the source text as compared to other types of adaptations. As Julie Sanders explains their difference in her theoretical work entitled *Adaptation and Appropriation*, she suggests: "[A]ppropriation frequently affects a more decisive journey away from the informing source into a wholly new cultural product and domain"(Sanders 2006: 27). Sanders's use of the term "appropriation" as if a different term outside adaptations has been criticised by certain adaptation studies scholars. In her seminal work entitled *Novel Shakespeares: Twentieth-Century Women Novelists and Appropriation*, Sanders discusses different understandings of the term "appropriation" with references to Daniel Fischlin and Mark Fortier's preference to use the word "adaptation", which sounds "less negative" as compared to "appropriation" in their edition of plays based on Shakespearean drama (Sanders 2006: 1, 2). Sanders quotes Fischlin and Fortier's argument that the term "appropriation" implies "a hostile take-over, a seizure of authority over the original" and juxtaposes their perspective with those of Christy Desmet and Robert Sawyer who read the same term as a sign of creativity and criticism (Sanders 2001, 1, 2). In *Novel Shakespeares: Twentieth-Century Women Novelists and Appropriation*, Sanders asserts that her use of the term broadly involves both "the process of textual take over and adaptation" (2001: 3).

When it is adaptations of canonical writers such as Shakespeare, this fidelity debate becomes even more explicit. It is now accepted by many literature authorities that the word Shakespeare no longer means the writer, and his texts basically imply a whole canon of literature. Therefore, adapting a canonical writer inevitably signifies an easier access to the heart of canonical issues or theoretical discussions on the one hand and a considerable challenge for a less known writer on the other. The idea of adapting Shakespeare, for instance, inevitably raises the questions of authority or authorship. In her groundbreaking work *A Theory of Adaptation*, Linda Hutcheon puts forth that adaptations of classics are usually "intended as tributes or as a way to supplant canonical cultural authority" (2006: 93). Most of the contemporary playwrights revisiting Shakespeare follow similar adaptive methods. They either own a loyal perspective foregrounding the significance of the Shakespearean source text or a challenging attitude towards Shakespeare, announcing that the adaptation is nearly an innovation, only inspired by the source text. In other words, adapting a canonical text in contemporary times usually implies either a yearning for the past or a search for alternating the past. However, in both cases, thematic intertextuality is often accompanied by an experimental form that the genre of adaptation inevitably accommodates. Borrowing Julie Sanders's words, adaptation is a "hybridized form" (2006:18) or a separate genre, which is the outcome of a metatextual encounter between past and present and between "continuity" and "difference" (Hutcheon 2001: 93). Therefore, adaptation owns a complicated ontological status, especially given the context of Shakespeare who metaphorically stands for the standards of dramatic form as well as a break away from the dramatic form of classical antiquity. In other words, reading Shakespeare requires an in-depth involvement in different modes of adaptation not only because we are still adapting Shakespeare in contemporary times but also because Shakespeare himself adapted the classical period. In this respect, it is necessary to remind the question Linda Hutcheon poses: do classical adaptations aim at "tribute[s]" or rather to "supplant the canonical figure of cultural authority"? (93).

The popularisation of adaptation studies goes in accordance with the contemporary movements. Especially the rise of postcolonial and feminist theories, which historically went parallel to the poststructuralist movements, have foregrounded the need for an alternative genre that would revisit the past with a new perspective. The counter-oppressive arguments provided by these discourses inevitably challenge the existing structures including the forms and genres of writing as well as the canon itself. While patriarchal and colonial contexts of many classical works are increasingly challenged in contemporary times, adaptation has proven itself as a very effective genre in communicating the desire to "dehistoricise" the past. Adaptation innately provides the dialectical form postcolonial and feminist theorists are urging as a host for "revision". Adrienne Rich defines "revision" as "an act of looking back, of seeing with fresh eyes, of entering an old text from a new critical direction—is for women more than a chapter in cultural history: it is an act of survival" and emphasises its significance for feminist criticism (2001: 18). Similarly, the postcolonial critic Henri Louis Gates addresses "revision" as a prerequisite for "signifying on" the major method for black semiotics, which, according to Gates, operates similar to adaptations, as "repeating with revising " (1988: 220–230). By the same token, adaptation studies has become the rising discipline of the last few decades, drawing on both comparative literature as well as interdisciplinary studies, and inevitably reinforced by oppression resistant discourses of contemporary times. In this respect, the idea of rewriting invites posthumanist readings of conventional texts while it also introduces a neutral form of discussion through its "hybrid" location in between the reader and the writer.

Reinforced by these inspiring theoretical discussions, this study explores intertextual dialogues, embedded in intergeneric forms, with a specific focus on the intercultural encounters accommodated in the in-between axis provided by extended intertextuality and postcolonial, feminist or posthumanistic texts. Given this context, Alice Walker's *The Color Purple's* intersemiotic journey into Steven Spielberg's film adaptation—with its postcolonial feminist stance—and Tom Stoppard's screen adaptation of his own drama play *Rosencrantz and Guildenstern Are Dead*, marked with hierarchical oppression consciousness; the indigenous adaptation processes in Yüksel Pazarkaya's Turkish Medea, *Mediha* and Ümit Kıvanç's *Macbeth: Muhitimize Uyarlama Denemesi* (*Macbeth: An Attempt to Adapt into Our Circle*), both of which display feminist concerns besides matters of cultural and geographical border; Welcome Msomi and Cherrie Moraga's postcolonial debates with the canon through Zulu Macbeth, *UMabatha*, and Mexican Medea, *The Hungry Woman*; as well as Djanet Sears and Jean Rhys's postcolonial feminist resistances through the form of prequel adaptations as seen in *Harlem Duet* and *Wide Sargasso Sea*, are all explored. Drawing on the antihierarchical relationship intertextuality announces by pointing out the dynamic axis between reading and writing, Sylvia Plath and Ntozake Shange's intertextual and intergeneric dialogues to reflect on their experimental forms in *Ariel* and *From Okra To Green* are examined under the light of posthumanist theory. In this respect, a discussion on posthumanist theories' connection to the idea of rewrite is also provided. Finally, two less studied works by Toni Morrison, namely "Recitatif" and *Desdemona,* are critically studied with a view to highlight their hybrid form, owing to multiple levels of readerly and writerly interactions, while guided by post-colonial theory, discussing the function of the form towards inclusivity. This study follows a comparative and an analytical method in providing close readings of these contemporary literary works while also offering a new perspective on intertextual relations, as guided by post-1960s theories, broadly focusing on oppression. This study contends to ask and discuss the underlying but long-neglected question of in what ways intertextuality connects to and/or responds to contemporary theories.

References

Aristotle. "Poetics". *Aristotle's Poetics*. Ed. O.B. Hardison. Trans. Leon Golden. Eaglewood Cliffs, NJ: Prentice Hall, 1968.

Barthes, Roland. *The Rustle of Language*. Berkeley: U of California P, 1989.

_____"Death of the Author". *Image, Music, Text*. Ed. and Trans. Stephen Heath. New York: Hill & Wang, 1978.

_____"Myth Today". *Mythologies*. Trans. Annette Lavers. New York: The Noonday P, 1972.

Braidotti, Rosi. "A Theoretical Framework for the Critical Posthumanities". Theory, Culture & Society. 36.6.31–61

Bloom, Harold. *The Anxiety of Influence: A Theory of Poetry*. New York: Oxford UP, 1997.

Derrida, Jacques. "The Law of Genre". www.sas.upenn.edu/12.06.2025.

Eliot, T.S. "Tradition and the Individual Talent". www.mat.msgu.edu.tr/ 15.06.2025.

Gates, Henri Louis. *The Signifying Monkey: A Theory of Afro-American Literary Criticism*. New York and Oxford: Oxford UP, 1988.

Hutcheon, Linda. *A Theory of Parody: The Teachings of Twentieth-Century Art Forms*. Champaign and Urbana: U of Illinois P, 2001.

_____ A Theory of Adaptations. New York: Routledge P, 2006.

Iser, Wolfgang. "The Reading Process: A phenomenological Approach". *Reader-response Criticism: From Formalism to Poststructuralism*. Ed. Jane P. Tompkins. Baltimore: Johns Hopkins UP, 1980.

Kristeva, Julia. "Word, Dialogue and The Novel". *Desire in Language: A Semiotic Approach to Literature and Art*. Ed. Leon S. Roudiez. Trans. Thomas Gora. New York: Columbia UP, 1980.

Lefevere, Andre. *Translation, Rewriting and the Manipulation of Literary Fame*. London and New York: Routledge, 1992.

Morrison, Toni. *Playing in the Dark: Whiteness and Literary Imagination*. Picador, 1993.

Pope, Alexander. "An Essay on Criticism". 1711.

Rich, Adrienne. "When We Dead Awaken: Writing As Revision". *College English*, 34.1, 1972: 18–30.

Sanders, Julie.. *Novel Shakespeares. Twentieth Century Women Novelists and Appropriation*. Manchester UP, 2001.

———— *Adaptation and Appropriation*. London and New York: Routledge, 2006

Strauss, Levi C. "The Structural Study of Myths". The Journal of American Folklore. V.68. No: 270. 428–444.

Wagner, Geoffrey. *The Novel and The Cinema*. Fairleigh Dickinson UP, 1975.

Whelehan, Imelda and Deborah Cartmell. Screen Adaptation. Impure Cinema. London and New York: Palgrave MacMillan, 2010.

Wordsworth, William. The Complete Poetical Works of William Wordsworth. Ed. Henry Reed. Philadelphia: Hayes & Zell, 1854.

Medea and Macbeth in Turkish: Ümit Kıvanç and Yüksel Pazarkaya's Cases of Indigenous Adaptations

The purpose of this paper is to examine two intercultural adaptations of canonical drama lending themselves to adaptations, namely *Medea* (480–406 BC) by Euripides and *Macbeth* (1606) by William Shakespeare in the contemporary Turkish context, with reflections on the idea of geographical and a spiritual border besides a feminist consciousness. While this study examines the late 1970s and 1980s' sociopolitical context issued in Ümit Kıvanç's *Macbeth: Muhitimize Uyarlama Denemesi* (1991) and Yüksel Pazarkaya's *Mediha* (1993) from a comparative perspective, it also revisits Linda Hutcheon's conception of "indigenous adaptations" (2006) with a view to highlight multiple layers of the two targeted intertextual engagements.

Since the terms "adaptation", "appropriation" and "rewrite" are often used interchangeably, a brief account of their conceptions within this study should be provided. This study draws on Linda Hutcheon's definition of the notion of "adaptation" as "an acknowledged transposition of a recognizable other work or works", including both "loyal" and "loose/free adaptations". Drawing on Daniel Fischlin and Mark Fortier's definition of "appropriation" as a "hostile take over, a seizure of authority over the other" (Fischin and Fortier 2000, 3) and Julie Sanders's description of the process as "a decisive journey away from the informing source into a wholly new cultural product and domain" (2006, 26), "appropriation" will be treated as a different category. Given this context, the study treats adaptive dialogue as "loyal" or "loose" in relation to the content added to or omitted from the source text. As for the notion of "appropriation", it is the political discourse or ideological perspective that determines it. The term "rewrite" is received broadly to involve intentional intertextual engagement with any previously published text.

The tragedy of *Macbeth* (1606), one of the Bard's timeless masterpieces, is an ever-adaptive play, the story of which is inspired by the historical account of *Macbeth*, King of Scotland, Macduff and Duncan, as recorded in *Holinshed's Chronicles* (1587). The script of Macbeth was also reworked by Shakespeare himself between its earliest stage recordings (1608) and its publication in the First Folio (1623). With its noteworthy adaptive potential, *Macbeth* has welcomed many intergeneric adaptations as novelised and screened versions, besides numerous stage adaptations by mainstream theater companies and well-known playwrights, including Charles Marowitz and Tom Stoppard.

As a contemporary Turkish playwright, Ümit Kıvanç rewrites *Macbeth* in Turkish as *Macbeth: Muhitimize Uyarlama Denemesi* (1991), transferring the context into that of the sociopolitical situation surrounding Turkey in the 1980s. Ümit Kıvanç, also recalled as the well-known TV presenter and humourist Halit Kıvanç's son, reads the protagonist as an ambitious politician who can easily sacrifice others for his own rise. Kıvanç's play can be considered a loyal adaptation in adhering to the Shakespearean plot and his poetic language. However, as Kıvanç transfers the story to search for power within political parties, he inevitably owns an ironic stance, which in turn shifts the source text genre (tragedy) to a comedy. He represents both the rise of Macbeth from the position of a party secretary to that of a party leader, and the fall of Macbeth as the army takes over the full control. Similar to the plot of Shakespeare's Macbeth, Macbeth's rise and fall are in accordance with the witches' prophecy. In order to assess Kıvanç's authorial dialogue with Shakespeare, it should be noted that he comes from an intellectual background and is an enthusiastic reader of Shakespeare.

Kıvanç's adaptive strategy in *Macbeth* targets writing a contemporary Turkish *Macbeth* rather than indigenising *Macbeth*. To exemplify, he renames certain characters authentically in Turkish, Başkurt, Lazkurt, Boşkurt, Özkurt (kurt, the Turkish name for wolf), while he keeps Macbeth and Lady Macbeth as Macbeth and Bayan Macbeth (exact translation for Lady Macbeth). King Duncan, whom Kıvanç transfers to the Party Leader, is called "Lider", while Banquo is called "Lazkurt", drawing on the ethnic origin of the character, coming from the North of Turkey, the Black Sea Region. Kıvanç's *Macbeth* is addressed as the southerner and recommended by the witches to "look towards the west rather than the east", which reinforces the play's underlying theme: Desire for power is independent of one's ethnic origin, as exemplified by "kurt's" coming from different regions all wishing to succeed Macbeth. Kıvanç stages a local Macbeth, underlining that the story of Macbeth is global. Yet Kıvanç's adaptive strategy offers no critique of Macbeth but rather of the Turkish politicians themselves through Macbeth. Kıvanç foregrounds the Turkish cultural context in the play. While the journalists who stand for the witches meet to discuss the recent news, they usually meet at a "kebapçı". Similarly, the "halay", a traditional Turkish folk dance, accompanies the exit of all the characters (the soldiers and the politicians) at the end. An innovative element is in Kıvanç's contemporary reading of the witches as media and their controlling power over the masses. Kıvanç translates the later prophecy of the witches in Macbeth that no man born from a woman can harm him into no elected man can ever succeed his situation to offer a critique on the military take over in the recent history of the Turkish Republic (1980s).

Kıvanç's major innovation is in shifting the genre from tragedy to comedy, which better accommodates his ironic stance towards the Turkish politicians. Kıvanç, therefore, is very careful in replacing violence with media scandals. For instance, unlike Duncan, Lider was not killed by Macbeth but was caught sleeping with a whore. He had to resign since his party lost its reputation and, in turn, a considerable percentage of votes. As General Hekate announces the military takeover, for instance, Macbeth utters these last lines, the irony in which contributes to the sense of comedy:

Never mind, my fellow,
These are the remnants of the Ottomans.
They will sure depart, having had their turn
And the moment comes
For people to celebrate our return.
Unless these guys sometimes appeared,
To make a dungeon out of Turkey,
Why would they re and reelect Macbeth,
The noble people of my country? (Kıvanç 1991: 13)

Merak etmeyin dostum,
Osmanlı artığıdır bunlar:
Küpünü doldurunca gider.

O vakit de aziz millet,
Bizim için bayram eder.
Hem arada bunlar gelip
Zindana çevirmese memleketi
Millet her seferinde göz göre göre
Yeniden seçer mi Macbeth'i? (1991: 14)*

* Based on the writer's Turkish to English translation of the quotation, which
appears on the book cover.

Based on the writer's Turkish to English translation of the following quotation, the major distinction between "cultural translation" and "intercultural
adaptation" can be noted as the writer's purpose, which, in turn, shapes
the rewriterly strategies owned. When stage translations or adaptations of
Shakespeare are considered, the "fidelity" issue becomes even more central in
determining the adaptive strategies of the adaptors. In her groundbreaking
work, *A Theory of Adaptation*, Linda Hutcheon puts forth that adaptations of
Shakespeare are usually "intended as tributes or as a way to supplant canonical cultural authority" (2006: 93). Most of the contemporary playwrights
revisiting Shakespeare either owns a loyal perspective, foregrounding the
significance of the Shakespearean source text or a challenging attitude towards
Shakespeare, announcing that the adaptation is nearly an innovation, only
inspired by the source text.

In order to better analyse the adaptive context of Kıvanç's plays, the
ongoing debate on the two intersecting concepts, "cultural translation" and
"intercultural adaptation", is noteworthy. As after 1960s, Translation Studies
dethrones the "source text-centered" approach and moves towards a "target
language- or target culture-centered approach", its new perspective is inevitably interrelated to Adaptation Studies, an interdisciplinary field emerging at
the same period. Given this context, the act of translation is also considered a
"rewrit[ing]" (Lefevere 1992: 8), and any theatrical performance is read as both
"stage translation" and "stage adaptation" (Bassnet-McGuire 1980: 107–128).

Linda Hutcheon and Julie Sanders's theories on adaptation are also related
to the levels of Ümit Kıvanç's adaptive dialogues with the Great Bard, while
their adaptive choices are treated within the context of what the celebrated
Shakespeare scholar, Graham Holderness, calls "the Shakespeare Myth"
(1988). "Shakespeare is here, now, always what is currently been made out
of him" (Holderness 1998: xvii). The above lines by Graham Holderness

are taken from his celebrated work, where he addresses Shakespeare as a "myth" (1988: xvii). William Shakespeare has become a name used nearly synonymously with World literary. His legacy foregrounds him as the most appropriated playwright, from the seventeenth century to ongoing contemporary times. It is now common knowledge that Shakespeare himself has used history and mythology as noteworthy references points in his drama. Ur-Hamlet and King Lear, for instance, were recycled from then-contemporary anonymous plays, while a considerable part of Othello was based on the sixteenth-century Italian writer Cinthio's short story Un Capitano Moro. Shakespeare's authorial revision has been a much-debated issue from 1725 onwards, from when Alexander Pope originally suggested that Shakespeare was a "double reviser" of both his own works and those of other writers in his *Preface to Shakespeare*, to our contemporary times. In her comprehensive study titled *Revising Shakespeare*, Grace Iopollo links "theatrical adaptation" to "authorial revision", relating the latter to Shakespeare's act in reworking his and his predecessors' works (1991: 20), usually after performance. Iopollo's suggestion reinforces the connection between the two words, "Shakespeare" and "revision".

It is now accepted by many literature authorities that the word Shakespeare no longer means the writer and his texts basically, but it has become an "icon". While being revisited by contemporary writers and critics, William Shakespeare is often depersonalised and "virtual"[ized] (Fischlin and Fortier 2000: 17), having become a signifier for the canon as well as a noteworthy reference for past and present modes and codes of representation. In other words, adapting Shakespeare inevitably signifies both an easy access to the heart of canonical issues or theoretical discussions on the one hand, and a considerable writerly challenge for a potentially canonical writer on the other. Borrowing Julie Sanders's words, adaptation is a "hybridized form" (2006: 18), or a separate genre, which is the outcome of a metatextual encounter between past and present, between "continuity" and "difference" (Hutcheon 2006: 93).

In other words, adapting Shakespeare in contemporary times usually implies either a yearning for the past or a search for alternating the past. However, in both cases, thematic intertextuality is often accompanied by an experimental form, which the genre of adaptation inevitably accommodates. Borrowing Julie Sanders's words, adaptation is a "hybridized form" (2006: 18), or a separate genre, which is the outcome of a metatextual encounter between past and present, between "continuity" and "difference" (Hutcheon 2006: 93). Therefore, adaptation owns a complicated ontological status, especially given the context of Shakespeare, who metaphorically stands for the standards of dramatic form, as well as a break away from the dramatic form of classical antiquity. In other words, reading Shakespeare requires an in-depth involvement in different modes of adaptation, not only because we are still adapting Shakespeare in contemporary times, but also because Shakespeare himself adapted the classical period. In this respect, it is necessary to recall the question Linda Hutcheon poses: do classical adaptations aim at "tribute[s]" or rather to "supplant the canonical figure of cultural authority"? (2006: 93).

As for Ümit Kıvanç, he owns a considerably loyal attitude in his dialogue with Shakespeare, although he adapts Macbeth freely. In his Afterword to the play, Kıvanç notes that his "loyal adaptation" of the Shakespearean play into the Turkish context should be thought of as stemming neither from his "arrogance" nor from his "desire to import a foreign play." Kıvanç relates his own motivation in adapting Macbeth to "a noble sense of unrest in witnessing that Turkey still lacks his long deserved Macbeth" (1991: 14). In revising *Macbeth* as *Macbeth: Muhitimize Uyarlama Denemesi*, he modestly calls his adaptive process "an attempt to adapt Macbeth into Shakespeare's Macbeth. our circle", which does not centrally accommodate "a seizure of authority" over Shakespeare.

Drawing on the myth of Jason and Medea, Euripides's canonical tragedy of *Medea* is a play lending itself to adaptations. The long list of its contemporary stage adaptations includes Toni Harrison's *Medea As A Sex-War Opera* (1985), Steve Carter's *Pecong* (1990), Cherríe Moraga's *The Hungry Woman: A Mexican Medea* (1995), Christa Wolf's *Medea* (1996), Marina Carr's *By the Bog of Cats* (1998), Liz Lochhead's *Medea* (2000), Caridad Svich's *Wreckage* (2011) and Neil LaBute's *Medea Redux* (2014).

The contemporary Turkish German playwright Yüksel Pazarkaya's *Mediha* (1993), a drama play written in Turkish and staged in Germany with simultaneous translation, offers a contemporary rewrite of Euripides's canonical tragedy, Medea, in a German-Turkish context. While revisiting the plot of Medea's betrayal by Jason through Glauke, *Mediha* displays a mainstream feminist gaze in questioning German Claudia's betrayal of Turkish Mediha more centrally than that of Turkish Jason, Hasan.

It is noteworthy to briefly address the playwright Yüksel Pazarkaya's background as a first generation of Turkish immigrants to Germany, where he had his BA in Philosophy and Literature. Pazarkaya's stage play incorporates the surrounding experience of the first-generation Turkish immigrants into Germany and Pazarkaya's observations of the social situation of Turkish immigrants in Germany during the late 1970s from the critical perspective of a humanities graduate. Pazarkaya's background in literature also reflects on the play's adaptive dialogue with Euripides's *Medea*, which accommodates this intentional and extended intertextual engagement on multiple levels of intercultural encounters. The adaptive context of Pazarkaya's drama play, *Mediha*, indeed, draws on the writer's observations of the social gap that the legislation before 1974 introduced in the specific cases of Turkish workers immigrating to Germany after the 1960s. Pazarkaya's *Mediha* not only transforms Euripides's *Medea*'s context of immigration from Colchis to Corinth into those of Turkish workers in Germany but also provides a valuable social critique.

To briefly visit the sociopolitical context concerning immigration from Turkey to Germany, the 1974 Legislation, under which many Turkish families had to live apart due to a man's employment in Germany, without settlement rights issued to their families, is an inevitable point of reference. For a considerable time, Turkish families had to find practical solutions such as fake marital arrangements for the sake of German citizenship, which implied their conception of the situation as temporary (Çelik 222–225), and introduced an even more difficult social process in adapting. *Mediha* centrally accommodates this significant sociopolitical issue of the time through Hasan's betrayal of Mediha with Claudia, pretending that he makes the choice of marrying Claudia as a practical path towards migration. Parallel to the lives of many immigrants, Hasan leaves his hometown to work in Germany and promises his family to unite afterwards.

Pazarkaya's *Mediha* also reflects a mainstream feminist stance in employing the issue of women's betrayal, the contemporary treatment of which is another significant sign of intercultural transfer. Unlike its source text, Euripides's *Medea*, Pazarkaya's play accommodates the encounter of Mediha and Claudia, the German woman, whom Mediha's husband, Hasan, intends to marry, as one major theme. In this respect, the intercultural transfer of the Nurse in Euripides's *Medea* to the Consultant woman (danışman kadın) in *Mediha* is noteworthy as it signals both the point of connection and that of departure between the two texts. While the Nurse undertakes the role of Medea's advisor in her experience of immigration from the city of Colchis to Corinth, as a consequence of Jason's choice to settle there, the Consultant Woman guides Mediha both socially and emotionally initially in her official process of application to and later in her social adaptation to Germany. In other words, one can observe *Mediha*'s strong connection to *Medea* through the underlying context of women's situation in man-made decisions of immigration, while also offering a significant point of departure in providing her individual story to fit into the notion of contemporary intercultural adaptations.

In accordance with the post-1960s trend among Anatolian villagers, Hasan leaves his hometown to start his job in Germany and promises to take his family afterwards. However, during the stages of his legal employment, Hasan is advised to marry Claudia, a German woman, in order to become a German citizen. In the meantime, Hasan's changing perception of women abandons him from Mediha and as he falls in love with Claudia. As Hasan decides to leave Mediha, she starts to experience isolation in a foreign land.

Homi K. Bhabha's notion of "hybridity" echoes in the text as Mediha's family finds itself at the state of "in-betweenness" (Bhabha 1994: 42–44), as two languages and two cultures encounter on multiple layers. Bhabha's notion of "cultural hybridity", the difficulty of which Bhabha points out (2), reflects on Mediha's experience as being Easterner and Westerner "at the same time" while being "neither the One nor the Other" (1994: 2–5). The form of the play reinforces this sense of in-betweenness through language shifts between Turkish and German. Drawing on phonetic similarity, Pazarkaya transfers Medea and Jason into the Turkish cultural context as Mediha and Hasan, while he also accommodates Glauke, more centrally, as the German Claudia. On the other hand, Mutlu Er suggests (2013: 25), Mediha's "soft and naive" personality is thoroughly different from that of Euripides's Medea. Pazarkaya's adaptive strategy foregrounds in his representation of Mediha as a prototype, standing for any rural Anatolian woman with low income and very limited education. As Hasan falls in love with the young and beautiful German woman, Claudia, and decides to leave the ageing Mediha, the play intertwines Euripides's plot and that of the 1972 Turkish film, *Dönüş* (*Return*), directed by Türkan Şoray. The naivety in the characterisation of Mediha is quite reminiscent of that of Gülcan in the movie, while there is an explicit parallelism between the two storylines. Like Hasan, İbrahim goes to Germany to work and falls in love with a German woman. Never going to Germany herself, Gülcan observes the changes in her husband from a distance, through his letters. Mediha, however, joins Hasan in Germany and experiences difficult incidents firsthand to finally witness Hasan's unexpected betrayal.

Mediha also incorporates East Anatolian folk language and elements into the play, as Pazarkaya chooses to use the word "yazgı", rather than the more common "kader", for "destiny". Similarly, Pazarkaya uses the rural Anatolian word "yazma", instead of "baş örtüsü", as Mediha covers her hair with a scarf. In a state of helplessness, Mediha also tries "kara büyü", an ancient Anatolian type of magic to evoke Hasan's love for her and eliminate her "kuma" (Pazarkaya 1993: 9), an East Anatolian concept for a man's second wife. In this respect, Pazarkaya's play draws on an "indigenization" (Hutcheon 2006: 150) of the witchcraft and poison for which the city of Kolchis is stereotypically known as Pazarkaya's "kara büyü". As Hutcheon suggests, "transcultural adaptations" often "indigenize" their source texts to "exert power over what they adapt" (2006: 150), especially when attempting to challenge and transform racial, ethnic and gender paradigms (2006: 147).

Mediha experiences a strong feeling of nonbelonging in Germany, where she loses her husband and experiences "the worst possible roof ever" ("bundan daha kötü dam olmaz") (Pazarkaya 1993: 59). The Female solidarity that she feels among other immigrant women in their visits to The Lady Consultant is her only safe ground for survival. Pazarkaya's unifying feminist concern echoes in the following lines of the group of immigrant women:

Hans, Hasan, Ali, Veli…
Erkeğe kaptırdın mı eli. / Once you give a man your hands (1993: 29);

Pazarkaya's *Mediha* represents an uneasy cultural encounter between the East and the West as embodied below from Mediha's own perspective: "My husband and my kids are my virtue. I am a woman. Let it be primitive or whatever, I am not selling my home" (Pazarkaya 1993: 19). Mediha's "namus", an East Anatolian saying for "women's honor and virtue", usually related to virginity before marriage and loyalty after marriage, is central to her personality; she would sacrifice anything to keep it. As a result, Pazarkaya makes sure to represent Mediha as a victim of patriarchal society as well as internalised patriarchy. Hasan finds her and the kids in a shelter, as decisive to deport Mediha from Germany. Mediha finally goes insane and kills her kids, not simply for revenge but because there is no exit. In other words, Mediha's "insanity" replaces "the social norm", which was hardly on the side of women (Yazıcıoğlu 2014: 35). In this respect, Pazarkaya's *Mediha*, by the end, is reminiscent of the earlier-mentioned argument on the disintegration of identity in Euripides's *Medea*.

As discussed above, *Mediha* centrally draws on the refugee context that is also present in Euripides' *Medea*:

> Women of Corinth, I have come outside to you.
> [...]
> You have a country. Your family home is here.
> You enjoy life and the company of your friends.
> But I am deserted, a refugee, thought nothing of
> By my husband—something he won in a foreign
> land (Euripides 1993: 214)

The above lines of Euripides's Medea highlight her growing sense of isolation as a "refugee" (1993: 214) from Colchis to Corinth. In her address to the women of Corinth, Medea frequently uses the pronouns "you" (plural) and "I", projecting her strong feeling of nonbelonging to this "foreign land" (1993: 214). There are also indicators of Medea's bodily and spiritual oppression, respectively, as she calls herself "deserted" (1993: 214), which implies that she yearns for her home, to contribute to her ambiguous state of self-perception as a foreigner.

The idea of rewriting a classical Greek text in Turkish, at first sight, implies an authorial debate with the canonical Greek writer Euripides—even more interesting if the sociohistorical and political dynamics of Turkish-Greek relations are considered—or a postcolonial stance towards the Western canon by "indigenizing" the cultural context of central Anatolia. The fact that Pazarkaya writes the play as an immigrant Turkish and German citizen himself and that the play was staged in Germany in Turkish to German simultaneous translation, overweighs the context, indeed. As the notion of any intertextual engagement also ontologically draws on the premises of an intercultural dialogue, its "in-between" process that runs on multiple levels to enable a "cultural translation", can metaphorically be accommodated at "the third space", where multiple identities will initially "clash", and then "co-exist" in a process towards "cultural negotiation" (Bhabha 1994: 225–227).

In its close examination of Ümit Kıvanç's Macbeth: Muhitimize Uyarlama Denemesi and Yüksel Pazarkaya's Mediha, this study contends that both drama plays read a certain historical period in Turkey, through their adaptive dialogues with the canonical tragedies of Macbeth and Medea. To conclude, drawing on Hutcheon's conception of "indigenous adaptations", it is possible to read Kıvanç's and Pazarkaya's innovative stage plays as "adaptations" rather than "appropriations", in the sense that Julie Sanders addresses the latter term. While Ümit Kıvanç's and Yüksel Pazarkaya's authorial dialogues remain considerably more loyal to Shakespeare and Euripides in building on and accrediting the source texts, both texts enable intercultural encounters by bringing into Macbeth and Medea, their contemporary, indigenous contexts. Apart from their adaptive modes, the two drama plays inevitably reassert Shakespeare's and Euripides's canonical situations, if not as authors, as original adaptors themselves.

References

Barthes, Roland. The Rustle of Language. Berkeley: U of California P, 1989.

Bassnet-McGuire, Susan. Translation Studies. London: Methuen, 1980.

Bhabha, Homi K. The Location of Culture. London, New York: Routledge, 1994.

Er, Mutlu. "Yüksel Pazarkaya'nın 'Mediha' Adlı Eserinde Türk Kadını İmgesi". Diyalog I (1). 24–31.

Euripides. Medea. Trans. Rex Warner. New York: Dover Thrift, 1993.

Fischlin, Daniel and Mark Fortier. "Introduction". Adaptations of Shakespeare. Ed. Daniel Fischin and Mark Fortier. New York: Routledge, 2000.

Gates, Henri Louis. The Signifying Monkey. A Theory of Afro-American Literary Criticism. New York and Oxford: Oxford Up, 1988.

Holderness, Graham (ed). The Shakespeare Myth. Manchester, New York: Manchester University Press, 1988.

Holinshed, Raphael. Holinshed's Chronicles of England, Scotland and Ireland. London: J. Johnson et al., 1807-08. (2nd ed. 1587)

Hutcheon, Linda. A Theory of Adaptations. New York: Routledge, 2006.

Iopollo, Grace. Revising Shakespeare. Cambridge, MA: Harvard UP, 1991.

Kıvanç, Ümit. *Macbeth: Muhitimize Uyarlama Denemesi.* İstanbul: İletişim Yayınları, 1991.

Lefevere, Andre. Translation, Rewriting and the Manipulation of Literary Fame. London, New York: Routledge, 1992.

Pazarkaya, Yüksel. *Mediha.* Ankara: Kültüt Bakanlığı Yayınları, 1993.

Pope, Alexander (ed). "Preface". The Works of Shakespeare. V1. London: 1725.

Sanders, Julie. Adaptation and Appropriation. London, New York: Routledge, 2006.

Shakespeare, William. Macbeth. The Arden Shakespeare. Ed. Kenneth Muir. (19th ed) London: Methuen, 1982.

Postcolonial Appropriations and Canonical Debates: Welcome Msomi's *Umabatha* and Cherrie Moraga's *The Hungry Woman: A Mexican Medea*

Cultural adaptations with strong postcolonial and feminist concerns often target debates with the canonical texts and prioritise this matter over adaptations themselves. The South African writer Welcome to Msomi's rewrite of Shakespeare's *Macbeth* in the Zulu context as *UMabatha* and Cherrie Moraga's postcolonial revisit of Euripides's Medea, titled *The Hungry Woman: A Mexican Medea*, can be considered "free postcolonial adaptations". Drawing on their strong discourses, I would like to consider these drama plays "postcolonial appropriations", borrowing the term "appropriations" from Julie Sanders, where she defines it as a "decisive journey away from the source text into a wholly new cultural product and domain" and agrees with Daniel Fischlin and Mark Fortier, who call such a process "a hostile take over, a seizure of authority" (Sanders 27).

The South African writer Welcome Msomi's Zulu *Macbeth, UMabatha,* was written in 1970 and first performed in 1971. The play follows a loose structure, adapting Shakespeare's *Macbeth* into the early nineteenth-century tribal Zulu culture. In *UMabatha*, Msomi's adaptive strategy is to juxtapose the similar stories of Macbeth and the Zulu chief Shaka, underlining that man's passion and ambition for power is a global and timeless issue. To put it in Nelson Mandela's words, "The similarities between Shakespeare's Macbeth and our [their] own Shaka become a glaring reminder that the world is philosophically, a very small place" (Fischlin and Fortier 2000: 165). Building on both Shaka's story, which is familiar to Zulu audiences and the worldwide known story of Macbeth, Msomi's play evoked not only local but also global interest, having been staged in South Africa, the United Kingdom

(Royal Shakespeare Company's Aldwych Theatre in London), Italy, Scotland, Zimbabwe, and throughout America.

UMabatha foregrounds the Zulu warrior culture by including South African Bantu warriors among its characters. The traditional Zulu music and dance employed on the background creates the effect that *UMabatha* is an African play. Another noteworthy element of intercultural transfer is explicit in Msomi's translation of *Macbeth*'s witches to the Zulu cultural context as the three Sandomas (heal doctors). The play follows the plot of *Macbeth* in a five-act play, which cuts some of the scenes and reduces some of the dialogues while echoing the most frequently quoted lines, such as:

> I have given suck, and know,
> How tender 'tis to love the babe that milks me:
> I would while it was smiling in my face,
> Have pluck'd my nipple from his boneless gums,
> And dash'd the brains out, had I so sworn,
> As you have done to this. (Shakespeare 1.7.55)

> Even if my own child was feeding at my breast/
> I would hurl him on to the rocks/
> And shatter his skull/
> Before I become as weak as you are now (Msomi 2000: 1.3)

On the other hand, Msomi's choice of juxtaposition as the adaptive strategy also signals a departure from the Shakespearean text. Given this context, *UMabatha* intends to provide more than an intercultural transfer since it offers a postcolonial perspective to *Macbeth* by rewriting a "white" play in a black context, as juxtaposed with a black story, that of Shaka. Msomi, for instance, is careful in referring to the sword as "assegai", with which Shaka was killed while following the fleeing clans. To quote Daniel Fischlin and Mark Fortier, "*UMabatha* decolonizes Shakespeare as a vanguard for colonial values, exposing the ways in which power and its abuses are not unique to colonial Western culture" (2000: 165). From a postcolonial perspective, Henry Louis Gates's conception of "signifying on" as a means of African American "revision" and "alteration" of White-centric canon is noteworthy. Drawing on the trickster figure "signifying monkey" in African vernacular, Gates traces the roots of black literary tradition to rhetorical or figurative "repetition" and "reversal", operating together through "doubling" (xv–xxv).

UMabatha's use of Zulu names linguistically similar to those of the source text, for characters such as Kamadonsela (Lady Macbeth), Dangane (Duncan), Bhangane (Banquo), Mafudu (Macduff), Makhiwane (Malcolm) and his addition of Zulu dancers, singers and warriors to the play, for instance, reflects his strategy to both "repeat" the Shakespearean play and "reverse" it as a non-Shakespearean, originally Zulu play.

It is, therefore, crucial to think about Msomi's choice of adaptation as a form of writing. Borrowing Julie Sanders's words, adaptation is a "hybridized form" (2006: 18), or a separate genre which is the outcome of a metatextual encounter between past and present, between "continuity" and "difference" (Hutcheon 2006: 93). Bringing a Homi Bhabhian postcolonial context to the conception of "hybridity", one can also read *UMabatha* as an intercultural encounter between the "colonizer" and the "colonized" (1994: 40–45). Fischlin and Fortier read *UMabatha* as a "complex series of cultural negotiations, appropriations, and meditations that define the relations between colonial and colonized cultures" (2000: 165). Given this context, adapting Shakespeare can be read as adapting a canonical English writer, rethinking Africa, dethroning the English context while remembering its effect, "renaming" *Macbeth* as *UMabatha*.

In order to assess his level of dialogue with the Bard, Welcome Msomi's background can be taken into consideration. As an enthusiastic reader of Shakespeare, Msomi's adaptive dialogue with Shakespeare is quite complicated. In his "Preface" to the play, Msomi notes that although he loved Shakespeare and had performed in several Shakespearean plays, he did not like the idea of adapting Shakespeare, "since I [he] felt I [he] was borrowing another writer's ideas" (165). Msomi's choice of the word "another writer" to refer to a canonical name as Shakespeare, can be taken as a denial of his canonical authority. Given this context, Msomi's *Umabatha* can be read as an "appropriation" of Shakespeare, a type of adaptation that Julie Sanders considers as "a decisive journey away from the source text into a new cultural domain", targeting "a seizure of authority over the original" (2006: 27).

As for the contemporary writers' level and intention of an intertextual dialogue with "the Great Bard", from the Elizabethan and Jacobean times, psychoanalytical perspectives on the issue of canonisation cannot be undermined. Given this context, it can be suggested that Welcome Msomi subconsciously contests with the "virtual" image of the globally canonical

Shakespeare, as contemporary writers, coming from literary traditions, not internationally canonised. In his celebrated work, *Freud and Man's Soul*, Bruno Bettelheim offers in-depth psychoanalytical readings of both *Oedipus* and *Hamlet* trace their paternal relations to signs of both rivalry and admiration. Bettelheim underlines the inevitability of this process, which takes place on an unconscious level (1983: 10–30). That the two protagonists cannot escape from the destined cycle resembles the restrictions of contemporary playwrights in responding to Shakespeare. In Harold Bloom's later psychoanalytical reading, "The largest truth of literary influence is that it is an irresistible anxiety. Shakespeare will never allow you to bury him, or escape him, or replace him. We have almost all of us, thoroughly internalized the power of Shakespeare's plays, frequently without having attended them or read them" (1997: xviii). Building on Bloom, one can consider Shakespeare an ever "precursor" for writers like Msomi and suggest that in an Oedipal pattern, any contemporary writer is doomed to end up repeating Shakespeare while yearning for a challenge and searching for his/her own candidacy for canonisation. Given the context of adapting Shakespeare, it is possibly the easiest way to start a literary battle with Shakespeare for many such new-generation writers whom Bloom would call "ephebe", stuck under the heavy anxiety of Shakespearean influence. "Resenters of canonical literature are nothing more or less than deniers of Shakespeare. They are not social revolutionaries or even social rebels. They are sufferers of the anxieties of Shakespeare's influence" (1997: xix). One can read Msomi's individual level of adaptive dialogue with Shakespeare within this context. However, Bloom's psychoanalytical theory of influence would account for neither the South African writer Welcome Msomi's collective source of inspiration in rewriting *Macbeth*, the story of Shakha, and his social motivation in revisiting a canonical play with postcolonial consciousness. Msomi's adaptive strategy in juxtaposition with *Macbeth* and the story of the Zulu chief signifies a canonical debate along with an intertextual and intergeneric dialogue.

The Chicana lesbian feminist playwright Cherrie Moraga employs a similar adaptive technique as she incorporates Euripides's canonical tragedy, *Medea*, and Aztec, Mayan myths of La Luna and La Llorona. As her title implies, Moraga announces her play *The Hungry Woman: A Mexican Medea*, prioritising La Llorona, the hungry woman, over Euripides's Medea. As a feminist activist, theorist, and playwright, Cherríe L. Moraga's challenge targets colonial as well as patriarchal codes embedded in literary texts. In her revolutionary play, *The Hungry Woman: A Mexican Medea*. Moraga innovatively incorporates Aztec and Mayan mythologies into Euripides's canonical tragedy. Moraga's play provides a Mexicanised version of Euripides's play, as reflected in her choice of the title. In her note to the drama play, Moraga foregrounds the Chicana background of her Medea, introducing her as "a leader in the Chicano revolt" (2003, 6). One can bring Hutcheon's context of "indigenizing" (2006, 150) into the reading of Moraga's drama play. Moraga's adaptive process involves an intercultural transfer in both content and form, while the adaptive strategy she undertakes goes beyond a cultural adaptation. Moraga brings a highly political context into her adaptation of *Medea*. To exemplify, Moraga revisits Medea's exile within the context of a Chicano revolt against the "oppressive" political and the economic system in the States (Moraga 2003, 6). Moraga also redefines the traditional Greek Chorus as distinctly "Cihuatateo": "a chorus of four warrior women warriors who, according to the Aztec myth, have died in childbirth" (2003, 8), with a note in her stage directions. The presence of an alternative Chorus becomes even more central as, wearing ancient skulls and barefoot, they perform traditional "Aztec *danzantes*" (2003: 8), accompanied by traditional Meso-American music. All these aspects can be viewed within Moraga's process of "indigenization" of Euripides's ancient Greek tragedy.

It should also be noted that Moraga's plot loosely adapts that of Euripides. The freely added content is that Moraga's Jason does not betray Medea, but, instead, Medea chooses her lesbian partner, Luna, over Jason, which in turn contributes to the revolutionary feminist context that the drama play offers. Similarly, the play omits some of Euripides's characters, all instrumental to the patriarchal context, such as Creon, Glauke and one of Medea's sons, and it adds original Chicana characters, three rebellious women, namely Luna, Mama Sal and Savannah.

Moraga's play announces itself as a distinctly Chicana text by rewriting Medea, Jason, the Nurse and Medea's son, now with the name Chac-Mool, as a Chicana character, while accommodating the themes of exile and child sacrifice within the Mexican-American context. Using the retrospective technique in revisiting Medea's time on exile, as accompanied by her son, Chac-Mool, and her lover Luna, Moraga puts an emphasis on the fact that they had to leave their homeland, Aztlan, for Phoenix. Moraga's plot successfully incorporates temporal shifts between past and present, in such a way as to evoke a sense of getting caught by the traumas of the past. Medea's yearning for Aztlan is a political signifier within the Mexican-American context. Indeed, its loss functions as a strong metaphor for their lost Aztec region, which later becomes a part of the "Gringo" land. The loss of Aztlan, a land of female warriors, also signifies the land's loss of connection with its maternal ties. The naming of Moraga's characters draws on Aztec myths as well. Chac-Mool implies a Pre-Columbian male figure, while Luna signifies the Aztec goddess Coyolxauhqui, who, according to the myth, was killed by their mother Coatlicue's (the Aztec goddess of creation and destruction) womb by her brother, Huitzilopochtli (sun god). Chac-Mool and Luna together represent Medea's embodiment of the myth of Coatlicue, since Luna stands for the Coyolxauhqui is the moon goddess, La Luna, whom one can only see partially due to the sun. According to the Aztec myth, the sun god, who is Luna's brother, cut her limbs and tossed her head in the sky (Moraga 2003, 160–162). Moraga employs this myth at the heart of her drama play, announcing their parallelism also in the stage directions in Act 2, with a note that Medea is in a dreamlike atmosphere, emerges from an icon and sweeps in the image of Coatlicue, simultaneously with Luna, who appears in the form of Coyolxauhqui (Moraga 2003, 55).

Haunted by unpleasant memories of the past surrounding Jason, Luna and Chac-Mool, Medea confesses that she killed her son to prevent Chac-Mool's process of becoming a "macho" (Moraga 2003, 6) and betraying his maternal roots metaphorically, through his inevitable sacrifice of Aztlan. In this respect, Moraga's Medea fits into the citizen identity which the Chicana theorist Gloria Anzaldúa (1999) defines as the one within "border" culture. Medea's experience of in-betweenness, failure in settling either in "Gringolandia" (USA) or in "Aztlan" (Mechicano country), as a Chicana subject, is the central context of Moraga's drama play. Given this context, "home" no longer implies a secure place but conveys the sense of defamiliarisation, as the following conversation between Savannah and Chac Mool puts forth:

SAVANNAH   And we made a kind of gypsy ghetto for ourselves in what was once a thriving desert.
MAMA SAL   They call it "Phoenix", pero entrenos, we name it "Tamoanchan", which means—
CHAC-MOOL We seek our home"
MAMA SAL   And the seeking itself becomes our home.   (Moraga 2003, 24)

Gloria Anzaldua's following lines reverberate their conversation by effectively capturing the essence of the Chicano experience of the "border", with an emphasis on its function in "splitting" between two places as well as two "pueblos":

> This is my home
> this thin edge of
> barbwire. (Anzaldúa 1999, 25)

In other words, this Chicano experience can be defined in relation to the border, which replaces their sense of home by becoming a strong metaphor for their ever-transitory act of settlement. As embodied in the metaphorical depiction of Aztlan, home can neither spatially nor spiritually be attained.

> BORDER GUARD: Where do you want to be?
> CHAC-MOOL: Aztlan. (Moraga 2003, 77)

It is also noteworthy that Aztlan signifies both masculine and feminine qualities of the "pueblo", as reinforced by Chac-Mool and Luna, Medea's past and present, respectively. Medea's in-between situation, due to her heterosexual past and queer present, can also be traced to multiple aspects of their encounter with the "border". Medea is indeed positioned in-between the margins of cultural definitions surrounding gender and ethnic identity, as well as the psychiatric state of "normal". Moraga's representation of Medea contributes to Anzaldúa's view of "borderline" as a fragmented experience (Anzaldúa 1999, 25–26). Medea's individual journey between codes of "heterosexual" and "queer", "postcolonial" and "decolonial" and "sane" and "insane" reflect on the dividing aspect of the border itself. Exiled from Aztlan both physically and spiritually, Medea experiences what Homi Bhabha calls "hybridity" and the difficulty of which he addresses as "neither the one nor the other while at the same time both the one and the other" (36). Bhabha also connects the "hybrid" experience to a state of "in-betweenness", announcing it as "third space" and attributing it the mission of intercultural "translation and negotiation" (1994, 40–43). The physical US-Mexico border also implies a spiritual border between two identities (Mexican and American) as well as two languages (Spanish and English). As for Moraga's adaptive strategy, her conscious departure from conventional forms of classical drama is explicit. That Moraga chooses a nonlinear and bilingual structure for her play, which acknowledges its central intertextual engagement with Euripides's tragedy, even by its title, is indeed a revolutionary stance. Moraga has once called her choice of a revolutionary form "a conscious deviation from Eurocentricism or Euro-Americanism"; an attempt to imagine "outside their structures" (Bilgin 2006, 134). Moraga's subversive dialogue with Euro-American "canon" becomes even more visible through her juxtaposition of the classical tragedy and Aztec, Mayan myths. In his celebrated work titled *Theatre of the Oppressed*, the Brazilian theatre critic Augusto Boal studies Aristotelian notion of theater and relates it to a state politics that suppresses individual "ethos" for the sake of implementing a "collective" one on the part of the audiences through "catharsis" and thus reinforcing conformity (Boal 2008, 1–4). Given this context, Moraga's adaptive method in appropriating Euripides's *Medea*, a canonical European text, imply a broader search for decolonisation. Adaptation accommodates interdisciplinary and intercultural encounters through intertextual and intergeneric dialogues with the canon. The postcolonial lesbian agenda, which Moraga brings into Euripides's classical tragedy and locates centrally with close links to pre-Columbian mythology, fits into what Julie Sanders calls an "appropriation" "a decisive journey, away from the informing source into a new cultural product and domain" (Sanders 2006, 26). *The Hungry Woman: A Mexican Medea* announces it's a subversion of mainstream stories and conventional forms by incorporating indigenous myths of "La Llorona" and "La Luna" more dominantly into Moraga's plot, while in constant dialogue with Euripides's canonical tragedy, *Medea*.

> Who are my gods? Who are my people? The response is the same for both both questions, I discovered, when I discovered the mutilated daughters of our indigenous American history of story: La Llorona, Coyolxauhqui, Coatlicue. I worship them in my attempt to portray them in all their locura, because I admire the living expression of their hungers... (Moraga 2003, Foreword)

The above lines by Cherrie Moraga explain her choice of *The Hungry Woman: A Mexican Medea* as the title by reflecting on the ever "hungry" state of Mexican Medea. The metaphor for hunger, indeed, stems from the myth of La Llorona, which deals with a woman with an unsatisfied desire for food. *The Hungry Woman: A Mexican Medea* revisits the Aztec myth of La Llorona with feminist consciousness. The ancient story is about the victimisation of a woman who constantly asks for food by male spirits, since she was different. The legend puts an emphasis on her mouth everywhere, "in her wrists", "in her elbows" and "in her ankles and knees" (Bierhost 1993, 23) To get rid of the hungry woman, who was unlike themselves, the male spirits initially try several violent techniques, none of which work. As they realise that La Llorona is still alive, despite their hard attempts, they also notice that the cycle of nature is on her side and somehow makes her survive: "When it rains, she drinks. When flowers shrivel, when trees fall, or when someone dies, she eats" (Bierhorst 1993, 25). Bierhorst notes that La Llorona is still so hungry that one can hear her cry for food and highlights that her story has not yet ended. In revisiting La Llorona's story, Moraga provides a strong Chicana feminist discourse. Moraga announces her thorough liberation of both Medea and La Llorona from surrounding patriarchal contexts by replacing the source text Medea's choice of hunger with self-torture by "hunger for food"; and thus, it reinforces Susan Bordo's reading of hunger as "a metaphor for sexual appetite" (110).

Moraga's major innovation is in her addition of her original Chicano(a) characters to *Medea* and her "revision" of colonial and patriarchal markers embedded in the classical tragedy, in the following sense that Adrienne Rich defines, in her inspiring study titled "When We Dead Awaken: Writing As Revision": "the act of looking back, of seeing with fresh eyes, of entering an old text from a new critical direction" and addresses as a means of "writing oneself back into history" (18) As Moraga juxtaposes the stories of Medea and Coatlicue, Luna and Coyolxauhqui in *The Hungry Woman: A Mexican Medea*, she celebrates a new, hybrid version of these stories with postcolonial and feminist consciousness. Beautifully captured through the extended metaphor "Aztlan", the search for home has become a Quixotic fight, as Luna notes, "Aztlan was uninhabitable" (Moraga 2023, 81). With the innovative form of adaptation, Moraga's drama play provides an in-between space for Gloria Anzaldúa's "los atravesdados", "forbidden inhabitants of the borderland", "those who cross over, pass over, or go through the confines of the 'normal'" (Anzaldúa 1999, 25) at the border of two texts, besides diegetic and mimetic genres of story and drama.

References

Anzaldua, Gloria. Borderlands: La Frontera. The New Mestiza. San Francisco: Aunt Lute Books, 1999 (1987).

Aristotle. "Poetics". Aristotle's Poetics. Ed. O.B. Hardison. Trans. Leon Golden. Eaglewood Cliff, NJ: Prentice Hall P, 1968.

Barthes, Roland. *The Rustle of Language*. Berkeley: U of California P, 1989.

Bassnet-McGuire, Susan. *Translation Studies*. London: Methuen, 1980.

Bettelheim, Bruno. *Freud and Man's Soul*. London: The Hogarth P, 1983.

Bhabha, Homi K. *The Location of Culture*. London and New York: Routledge, 1994.

Bierhorst, John. The Hungry Woman: Myths and Legends of the Aztecs. New York: Quill William Morrow P, 1993.

Bloom, Harold. *The Anxiety of Influence: A Theory of Poetry*. New York: Oxford University Press, 1997.

Boal, Augusto. Ezilenlerin Tiyatrosu. Çev. Necdet Hasgül. İstanbul: Boğaziçi Üniversitesi yayınları, 2008.

Bordo, Susan. Unbearable Weight: Feminism, Western Culture and the Body. London: U of California P, 1995.

Euripides. Medea. New York: Dover Thrift P, 1993.

Fischlin, Daniel and Mark Fortier. "Introduction". *Adaptations of Shakespeare*. Ed. Daniel Fischin and Mark Fortier. New York: Routledge, 2000.

Gates, Henri Louis. *The Signifying Monkey. A Theory of Afro-American Literary Criticism*. New York and Oxford: Oxford Up, 1988.

Holderness, Graham (ed). *The Shakespeare Myth*. Manchester, New York: Manchester University Press, 1988.

Hutcheon, Linda. *A Theory of Adaptations*. New York: Routledge, 2006.

Iopollo, Grace. *Revising Shakespeare*. Cambridge, MA: Harvard UP, 1991.

Lefevere, Andre. *Translation, Rewriting and the Manipulation of Literary Fame*. London, New York: Routledge, 1992.

Miller, J. Hillis. "Ariachne's Broken Woof". *The Georgia Review*. vol. 31, no. 1, year, p. 44–60.

Moraga, Cherrie. The Hungry Woman: A Mexican Medea and Heart of the Earth. A Popul Vuh Story. New Mexico: West End P, 2003.

_____. " A Challenge to Borderline From A daughter of Aztlan: An Interview With Cherrie L. Moraga. Ed. İnci Bilgin. JAST. "Special Chicana/o Issue. Eds. Ayşe Lahur Kirtunç and Maria Herrera Sobek. V23. Spring 2006. İzmir, Ege UP.

Msomi, Welcome. "UMabatha". Adaptations of Shakespeare. Ed. Daniel Fischin and Mark Fortier. New York: Routledge, 2000.

Rich, Adrienne. "When We Dead Awaken: Writing As Revision". College English. 34.1. 1972: 18–30.

Pope, Alexander (ed). "Preface". The Works of Shakespeare. V1. London: 1725.

Sanders, Julie. Adaptation and Appropriation. London, New York: Routledge, 2006.

Shakespeare, William. Macbeth. The Arden Shakespeare. Ed. Kenneth Muir. (19th ed) London: Methuen, 1982.

Welcome, Msomi. "UMabatha". Adaptations of Shakespeare. Ed. Daniel Fischin and Mark Fortier. New York: Routledge, 2000.

Intersemiotic Journeys Through the *Color Purple* and *Rosencrantz and Guildenstern Are Dead*

This part looks at the intersemiotic processes of the celebrated novel, *The Color Purple*, by the contemporary black feminist writer, Alice Walker, and the well-studied drama play, *Rosencrantz and Guildenstern Are Dead*, by the British playwright Tom Stoppard, was through in 1985 and 1991 screen transfer journeys, with a view to highlight how their postcolonial feminist and anti-hierarchical concerns, respectively, find their forms. In his ground-breaking study titled *Film and Theatre (The Literature of Cinema)*, Allardyce Nicoll argues that screen adaptation of novels often implies a less complicated transfer process as compared to drama plays (1936: 172–175). To start with, that both the language and method of cinema are thoroughly different from that of literature should be acknowledged.

The screen adaptation of a novel implies an intergeneric transfer from diegetic to mimetic mode as well as from the textual narrative's diegetic to the cinematic narrative's diegetic mode, and thus, it can be subject to a considerable loss of certain strong narrative techniques. On the other hand, theater to film transfer indicates a difficulty owing to theater and cinema's different understandings of "showing" (Hutcheon 2006: 44–45).

Contemporary American novelist Alice Walker's Pulitzer Prize-winning novel *The Color Purple* has been subject to both postcolonial and feminist critics' interests for its thematic engagement with the sorrowful life of Celie, a black female character in the post-civil war states, whose life starts with parental rape and continues with male betrayal till late adulthood. The novel's dialogue with the bildungsroman tradition in depicting Celie's traumatic experiences as surrounded by her pathological father and machoic husband as well as its incorporation of letters within the narrative reminiscent of the eighteenth-century tradition of the epistolary novel has also appealed to contemporary critics' interest. The novel goes through two screen-friendly adaptation processes, initially as directed by Steven Spielberg in 1985 with Whoopi Goldberg playing Celie, where the film was shortlisted for the Oscar Award in 11 different categories and a second time in 2023, as directed by the Ghanaian filmmaker Blitz Bazawule, to meet its spectators, with a note under the same title as "a bold new take on the beloved classic". This study examines Walker's *The Color Purple* not with a focus on the postcolonial feminist stance, but it consistently takes with a closer perspective to its form, as surrounded by a discussion on the semiotic system for which the novel is perpetually adaptive and forever contemporary. Given this context, this study draws on Henri Louis Gates's suggestion of a particular black semiotic system operating in literary texts written by black writers and by "signifying on" its own tradition of writing (1988: 56, 57).

The strongest components of Celie's story are the letters interwoven into her narrative, in accordance with the tradition of the epistolary novel. Celie starts to write letters as soon as she learns how to read and write, following the hints she was previously given by her beloved sister, Nettie, before the Father forced Nettie to leave. As the heroine Celie addresses her letters initially to God and subsequently to her sister Nettie to share her sorrow, the narrating Celie indirectly addresses the second-level witness, her implied reader, with a strong narrative device. Steven Spielberg's film *The Color Purple* (1998) transfers these narrated parts as dramatic action incorporated with the flashback technique, while the letters in which Celie initially addresses God and then Nettie are central to the novel's plot. On the contrary, the novel and the film share the common involvement of strong visual signs. The novel's consciousness of visuality is reflected through reference to individual letters composing single words; in other words, a treatment of the letters as a linguistic set of signifiers. On the other hand, the film is a different genre, which operates through "showing" rather than "telling"; and thus, it celebrates the images and visuality even more than the adapting content of the novel. The verbal language, which is the only possible authorial grasp of a visual sign, remains an auditory sign in the film version.

The novel's intergeneric potential in creating visual images in its readers' minds through the letters, which are themselves also a linguistic set of visual signifiers, is also noteworthy. Yet stylistic reflections on the language, which enable any possible authorial grasp of visual sign, remain an auditory sign in film transfers. For instance, the naming of Celie's husband as "Mister" implies his being reduced to a patriarchal prototype to project his oppressive attitude towards his wife. Mister stands for the overall context of patriarchy involving all its codes and stereotypes. For the reader, the word "mister", which is a combination of the letters "m-i-s-t-e-r", is also a visual signifier, especially reflecting on Celie's process to become literate. When Nettie teaches Celie how to read and write, she makes use of surrounding objects over which she writes the individual letters composing the words. This teaching technique implies a signification on the signifying chain of language itself by underlining how stylistic and semantic levels can operate as delayed in their inevitable match. Similarly, the letters Celie has been writing to Nettie in the novel, which are the only access of narration for the reader, are visual signifiers of their communication or lack of communication:

Dear Nettie,

The only piece of mail Mr...... ever put directly n my hand is a telegram that come from the United States, Department of Defense. It say the ship you and the children and your husband left Africa in was sunk by German mines off the coast of some place called Gibralta. They think you all drowned. Plus, the same day all the letters I wrote to you over the years come back unopen. I sit here in this big house by myself trying to sew, but what good is sewing gon do? What good anyting? Being alive begin to seem like a awful strain.

Your sister,
Celie (1985:262).

Given this context, the letters function outside their accustomed association as encoded messages sent by the sender to a recipient to decode. Since the letters cannot be received due to mister who receives Nattie's letters instead of the expected recipient, Celie, the chain of signification is broken. Letters become a tool not for communication but for discommunication. Until Celie finally receives the letters with the help of Shug Avery, there has been a great delay in time, which relocates the letters to be signifiers of loss and delay. Similarly, another incorporated narrative, the telegram, which passes the news of Nettie's death, signifies miscommunication, disintegrating the accustomed association of the telegram with communication. As Rimmon-Kenan suggests, "Story as a construct and an abstraction from the set of possible signifiers (text), is intangible within itself" (1999: 7). In this respect, the reader and the audience of *The Color Purple* are after different but both instrumental signifiers to catch the "master signifier" (2006: 695). As the title "The Color Purple" is a signifier without any specific reference, both the audience and the reader struggle to receive the message and meaning embedded in this code. Roland Barthes defines codes as follows: "The code is a perspective of quotations, a mirage of structures, so many fragments that has been already read, seen, done, experienced; the code is a wake of that already" (1974, 20). What *The Color Purple* signifies in the given context becomes the central question of both texts. However, even in the limited context of the texts, both the reader and the audience are to choose one among a set of possible signifieds. In his celebrated essay "The Death of the Author", Roland Barthes considers reading a sort of writing that requires producing the texts' signifiers by allowing them to be caught up in the network of codes with a final signified (1977, 147). As the reception theory offers, bringing their own background into their individual receptions of the text, each and every reader or audience can interpret the text differently. Besides, in subsequent reading or watching experiences, one's focal point and, in turn, his/her perceptions of the text can change. In his inspiring study entitled "Interactions Between Text and Reader", Wolfgang Iser notes that "the reader's communication with the text is a dynamic process of self-correction, as he formulates signifieds which he must then continually modify" (1980: 111–112). In other words, that would be an in vain attempt to fix a specific signifier to a single signified, while the process of signification is innately ongoing.

While Celie's sad story progresses in the timeline, Celie's narration calls the shadow reader to play a game with instrumental signifiers, projecting the reader's overall struggle with the master signifier embedded in Walker's title. Since, outside the reading process, "The Color Purple" stands as a signifier without a particular reference, it reinforces Henri Louis Gates's suggestion of "signifying on" as a black semiotic process, responding to the African oral tradition of trickster and projecting in black literature (1988: 55–58). In one of the African myths of the trickster, the monkey challenges the authority of the lion by using the elephant as an instrument. While the lion takes all the monkey's words on the literal level, the monkey signifies on the language as he undertakes a figurative level of speech. The monkey ends up humiliating both the lion and the elephant by causing an argument through an intended miscommunication the monkey starts between the two. As the lion and the elephant take the monkey's words on the literal level, the signifying monkey indeed signifies on language through which he dupes them. Gates's argument draws on his observations on the black tradition of writing, where the signifying layer of figurative language stands in between the signifier and the signified and functions as continuous repetition with a revision (1988: 56). In this respect, Alice Walker's novel provides an innovative form of intergeneric dialogue by signifying on the conventional signification process and doing this while revisiting the tradition of epistolary novel at the same time.

Despite its placement in the title, neither the novel nor the film involves any reference to "purple". On the other hand, the notion of colour has functioned as a significant sign in both texts, since most of the characters are coloured:

They calls me yellow
like yellow be my name

They calls me yellow
like yellow be my name

But yellow is a name
Why ain't black the same

Well, if I say Hey black girl
Lord, why she try turn ruin my game (1985: 104)

Colour is not only depicted or represented as a racial sign for blackness but also as a sign of unpleasant memories. When *The Color Purple* is read as a sign within the African American context, it corresponds to the colourful image of Africa with vast ophia, which Spielberg's film greatly reinforces with its scenes of memories on Africa. The colour red can also be read as a signifier of the African blood, which is visible in the cheek (Hurston, 1928), and the colour blue can be taken as a signifier of an escape from the reality of African experience of slavery, as embedded in blues, the lyrics of which are sorrowful in contrast to its fast rhythm. Colours red and blue together form purple and make up for the dual African American identity, which Du Bois states long ago: "Negro is sort of the seventh son, born with a veil and gifted with second sight... this sense of looking at oneself through the eyes of the other" (1961: 2).

Another possible connotation of colour purple would be irreconcilable memories surrounding the heroine Celie and her female companions, Nettie, Sophia and Shug. In this respect, the female characters can be classified as the submissive and rebellious ones. While Shug, Sophia and Nettie wear clothes with strong colours signifying passion, Celie's colour is usually blue, which signifies sorrow and reminds her of blues. Providing scenes where the incorporation of the African experience and female companionship are accompanied by blues and colourful images to finally reinforce both contexts together visually and auditorily, Steven Spielberg's film captures the colour purple through the audience's sensory perception. Norman Bryson suggests that even in each context "the sign acquires its meaning from the place it projects itself forward to, or lands in" (99). Similarly, Keir Elam considers the performance text as a macro-sign, the meaning of which is constituted by the total effect (1980: 7).

In other words, *The Color Purple* invites its readers and audiences into an intersemiotic play, while at the same time reinforcing the consciousness that there are stories or narrative units embedded in signs. Through their intergeneric emphases, Walker's novel and Spielberg's film reflect on the following question, if not suggestion, by Roland Barthes: "Can the process of signification ever be closed within the text itself" (1974: 10).

The British playwright Tom Stoppard's celebrated drama play *Rosencrantz and Guildenstern Are Dead* (1966), a rewrite of Shakespeare's *Hamlet* in the form of existential comedy, has had a highly acclaimed stage history ever since its premiere in Edinburgh Fringe in 1966. Tom Stoppard himself adapted the play to screen in 1990, adding the following modest note: "—at least the director wouldn't have to keep wondering what the author meant. It just seemed that I'd be the only person who could treat the play with the necessary disrespect" (Brunette, 1991).

In revisiting Rosencrantz and Guildenstern, the two minor characters of Shakespeare's *Hamlet*, so central that they become the protagonists of the new drama play, Stoppard's "free / loose adaptation" or "appropriation" offers a social critique on the hierarchical representations in *Hamlet*. However, echoing several other cinema critics, the well-known film critic Roger Ebert considered the stage to screen transfer problematic and noted that "this material…can hardly work as a film" (1991). Constance J. Gianakaris' words, "motion pictures are primarily … a visual medium; theatre is primarily … verbal, hence largely metaphoric" (1985: 85), point out the intersemiotic transfer from theatre to cinema as difficult. Similarly, the adaptation studies theorist Linda Hutcheon considers drama on screen as a complicated transfer owing to the copresence of "two different modes of showing" (2006: 46–50).

Tom Stoppard's film, *Rosencrantz and Guildenstern Are Dead*, is a loyal screen adaptation of his own drama play, where Stoppard reimagines Rosencrantz and Guildenstern in an Absurdist three-act play. In *Rosencrantz and Guildenstern Are Dead*, the duo is represented in an attempt to be the major characters while the Shakespearean plot remains in the background, evoking intertextual consciousness. *Rosencrantz and Guildenstern Are Dead* specifically revisits Acts 4 and 5 in *Hamlet*, where Claudius commissions Rosencrantz and Guildenstern to find out the reason for Hamlet's bizarre actions and finally entrap him. As Hamlet learns the plan and changes the content of the letter, which orders his own execution into theirs, Rosencrantz and Guildenstern get executed instead of Hamlet. This overall existential questioning reflects on Stoppard's script through in-depth questionings of man as opposed to fate, as signified by Rosencrantz and Guildenstern's struggle to survive against Shakespeare's plot.

The scene opens as Rosencrantz and Guildenstern ride their horses to Elsinore, getting involved with absurd discussions on the rule of probability as they find a coin that constantly comes up heads. They encounter a group of players, and as they start a conversation with them, they find themselves in the middle of Hamlet's plot. That they desperately try to understand the given circumstances in Hamlet by eavesdropping on the characters' conversations contributes to the sense of a dark comedy. As assigned by the king and the queen, the two are sent to deliver a letter to England by ship. There, they learn the content of the letter and try pretending they did not see the letter. As in Shakespeare's play, Hamlet replaces the letter and escapes on another ship. Ignorant of the situation, Rosencrantz and Guildenstern eventually get hung by the players and the tragedians get ready for the rest of their journey.

Both Stoppard's play and film follow the tradition of the theatre of the Absurd in giving the audience a sense of circular plot, reminiscent of Rosencrantz and Guildenstern's repetitive existential questionings of life:

Ros: Heads.
(He picks it [the coin] up and puts it in his bag. The process is repeated.) Heads.
(Again.)

Heads. (Again) Heads. (Again) Heads.

Guil: (Flipping a coin) There is an art to the building up of suspense. Ros: Heads.
(Stoppard 1967: 9)

Overrepetition in the word "heads" becomes disturbing to the film audience as well as the repetitive conversations on the rules of probability. "Time has stopped dead, and the single experience of one coin being spun once has been repeated ninety [in the film version a hundred and fiftysix] times" (1967: 12). That the death of Rosencrantz and Guildenstern hardly makes any difference either in Shakespearean text or in Stoppard's text or in real life is the underlying message to contribute to the overall existentialist context.

The self-reflexive and intertextual qualities of Stoppard's play are revisited in the screen adaptation, also to reinforce the existentialist context, by offering a reading of the Shakespearean source text as Rosencrantz and Guildenstern's inevitable fate. Similarly, the major player keeps reminding Rosencrantz and Guildenstern of the conventional rules of theatre, which reflects on the fact that Stoppard's is an unconventional drama play. References to the stage create a sense of stage-consciousness in the audience, which, in an intersemiotic transfer, evokes a sense of intertextuality as well. Another noteworthy example of metatextuality is that Rosencrantz and Guildenstern start their boat trip right after watching *The Murder of Gonzago*, an already existing self-referential and intertextual device in Shakespeare's *Hamlet*, as performed by the players. In this respect, the play-within-play structures of both *Hamlet* and *Rosencrantz and Guildenstern Are Dead* are revisited in the film with an intergeneric consciousness, with references to *Hamlet*'s well-known Hollywood production. The falling pages of Shakespeare's script before Rosencrantz and Guildenstern meet the characters of *Hamlet* is not only a foreshadowing of the upcoming encounter but also a strong cinematic technique to reflect on the adaptive process itself.

Stoppard's text also positions Rosencrantz and Guildenstern as a double rather than individual identities, the latter of which is Allardyce Nicoll's suggestion for the cinematic mode. To add to their prototypical characterisation and to contribute to their dual reception, Rosencrantz cannot distinguish between himself and Guildenstern as he frequently confuses the two names. In an interview, Eugene Ionesco reads "puppet show" as the essence of both Absurd theatre and life (web), which, in turn, accounts for the puppet-like representations of Rosencrantz and Guildenstern. Always controlled by macrocosmic forces and frequently limited in action and comprehension, Rosencrantz and Guildenstern are more similar to puppets than individuals.

Susan Sontag's question "[i]s cinema the successor, the rival, or the revivifier of theatre?" projects the intergeneric relations between two methods, both of which draw on "showing" (1985: 371). Juxtaposition of two different understandings of showing can indeed introduce a major challenge. Showing plays an instrumental role in theatre, whereas it is very essential to cinema. Theatre rather operates through signs. Keir Elam notes that the presence of signs on stage "suppresses the practical function of phenomena in favour of a symbolic or signifying role" (1980: 6). In this respect, the signifying process itself is the essence of theatrical reception, while screening a play implies a challenging intersemiotic transfer since the language of cinema is more vision oriented.

In Allardyce Nicoll's words, "The theatre rejoices in artistic limitation in space while the film demands movement and change in location" (1936: 173). Susan Sontag, similarly, states, "Movies are regarded as advancing from theatrical artificiality to cinematic naturalness and immediacy" (1985: 340). In other words, characteristically, cinema can easily explore a dynamic context while representing a static situation usually becomes a challenge on screen, unlike on stage. The double adaptation process may be another challenge for the film to consider. Stoppard's film draws on an "appropriation "of Shakespeare's *Hamlet* and its screen transfer. The term "appropriation" should also be distinguished from other adaptive modes:

"[A]ppropriation frequently affects a more decisive journey away from the informing source into a wholly new cultural product and domain" (Sanders 2006: 27). Stoppard's adaptive strategy in loosely revisiting *Hamlet* is manifested in the existentialist context he addresses as well as his choice of postmodern techniques of self-referentiality and intertextuality. By nature, Stoppard's text *Rosencrantz and Guildenstern Are Dead* implies a shared authority on multiple layers as an appropriation of Shakespeare's canonical play, in turn both an adapting and adapted text. This complicated ontological situation reflects on the following dialogue between Rosencrantz and Guildenstern:

> Guil: (Seizing him violently) WHO DO YOU THINK YOU ARE?
>
> Ros: Rhetoric! Game and match! (Pause.) Where's it going to end?
>
> Guil: That's the question.
> Ros: It's all questions.

When the structural qualities of the play are directly transferred, without being adapted into a new medium as cinema, the film conveys the sense of a screened stage, which is not very favourable to screen audiences. Given this context, Jean Mitry's strategy for adapting theatre to film is finally reinforced: "[...] the play would become something altogether different. It would take on another meaning, open onto different perspectives, because the means of expression in being different would express different things-not the same things in different ways" (1971: 1).

Consequently, it should be noted that in both novel-to-screen and drama-to-screen adaptations, the adaptation itself should be viewed as a new product of the intergeneric encounter. In Robert Stam's words, film adaptations "are caught up in the ongoing whirl of textual reference and transformation, of texts generating other texts in an endless process of recycling, transformation, and transmutation, with no clear point of origin" (Stam, 2000: 66). In other words, the open invite for intergeneric dialogues and the levels of the textual encounters, both of which are different and none of which is original, designates the strength of the adaptation itself. Despite numerous criticisms arguing for fidelity to source texts in screen adaptations, Susan Sontag suggests that the strength of a film adaptation depends on how far it gets away from its source text (Sontag 1985: 348). In this respect, what lies beneath a more successful translation of *The Color Purple*, as compared to *Rosencrantz and Guildenstern Are Dead*, can be addressed as the adaptation being granted its own aura, as a consequence of an open process of intersemiotic dialogues.

References

Albee, Edward. *The Zoo Story and Other Plays*. London: Penguin, 1995.

Albee, Edward. "Which Theatre Is The Absurd One?" *The Modern American Theater.* Ed. Alvin B. Kernan. Eaglewood Cliffs, N.J: Prentice-Hall, 1967.

Barthes, Roland. *S/Z.* Trans. Richard Miller. New York: Hill and WAg, 1974.

———. *Image /Music/Text.* Trans. S. Heath. London: Fontana P, 1977.

Bassnet, Susan. *Translation Studies.* London, New York: Routledge, 1991.

Brunette, Peter. "Stoppard Finds the Right Man to Direct His Film". *The Los Angeles Times.* 20 February 1991.

Bryson, Norman. "Semiology and Visual Interpretation". *Reading Images.* Ed. Julia Thomas. New York: Palgrave P, 2001.

Du Bois, W.E.B. *The Souls of Black Folk: Essays and Sketches.* Ed. Saunders Redding Greenwich. Conn: Fawcett, 1961.

Ebert, Robert. "Rosencrantz and Guildenstern Are Dead". *Chicago Sun-Times.* 15 March 1991.

Elam, Keir. *The Semiotics of Theatre and Drama.* London; New York: Methuen, 1980.

Esslin, Martin. *The Theatre of the Absurd.* Penguin, 1972.

Gates, Henry Louis. *The Signifying Monkey: A Theory of Afro-American Literary Criticism.* New York: Oxford UP, 1988.

Gianakaris, Constantine J. "Drama into Film: The Shaffer Situation." *Modern Drama* 28, No. 1 (1985): 83–98.

Hobson, Harold. A Fearful Summons. *Sunday Times.* 16 April 1967, 49.

Hurston, Zora Neale. "How It Feels To Be Colored Me". www.scalar.lehigh.edu/10.06.2025.

Iser, Wolfgang. "Interaction Between Text and Reader". *The Reader In the Text: Essays On Audience and Interpretation.* S.R. Suleiman and I. Crosman, eds. Princeton: Princeton UP, 1980.

Lacan, Jaques. "The Subversion of the Subject and the Dialectic of Desire in the Freudian Unconscious" *Ecrits the First Complete Edition in English.* Trans. B. Fink. New York, London: Norton P, 671–702.

Mitry, Jean. "Remarks on the Problem of Cinematic Adaptation". *The Bulletin of the Midwest Modern Language Association,* Vol. 4, No. 1. (Spring, 1971). 1-9.

Nicoll, Allardyce. *Film and Theater.* Thomas Y. Crowell, 1936.

Pavis, Patrice. *Languages of the Stage: Essays in the Semiology of the Theatre.* New York: Performing Arts Journal Publications, 1993.

Rimmon-Kenan, S. *Narrative Fiction: Contemporary Poetics.* London and New York: Routledge, 1999.

Rivlin, Elizabeth. "A Tom Stoppard Film: agency and adaptation in *Rosencrantz and Guildenstern Are Dead*." *Modern British Drama on Screen.* Ed. R. Barton Palmer and William Robert Bray. Cambridge: Cambridge U.P, 2013.

Sanders, Julie. *Adaptation and Appropriation.* London, New York: Routledge, 2006.

Sartre, Jean Paul. *Existentialism Is A Humanism.* Yale U.P, 2007.

Shakespeare, William. "Hamlet". *Tragedies.* London: Marshall Cavendish, 1998.

Sontag, Susan. "Film and theatre". *Film Theory and Criticism.* Ed. G. Mast and M. Cohen. 1985.

Spielberg, Steven. *The Color Purple* (film). Warner Bros, 1985.

Stam, Robert. "Beyond Fidelity: The Dialogics of Adaptation". *Film Adaptation.* Ed. J. Naremore. 2000, 54–76.

Stoppard, Tom. *Rosencrantz and Guildenstern Are Dead.* London: Faber and Faber, 1967.

————. *Rosencrantz and Guildenstern Are Dead* (film). 1990.

Walker, Alice. *The Color Purple.* New York: Pocket Books P, 1985.

Postcolonial Feminist Resistance and Prequel Adaptations: Jean Rhys's *Wide Sargasso Sea* and Djanet Sears's *Harlem Duet*

This part examines *Wide Sargasso Sea* and *Harlem Duet* with a view to highlight the specific function of prequel adaptations as modes of postcolonial feminist resistance. The feminist theorist Adrienne Rich's feminist call for "revisioning" has often been well responded to by contemporary feminist writers, especially those coming from an indigenous background. While Rich points out the significant function of "revisioning" by calling the process of "entering an old text from a new critical dimension", an attempt to write themselves back into history (Rich 1992). As a hybrid genre enabling a dialogue between a canonical and a noncanonical text besides their contextual relations to past and present, adaptation often invites postcolonial and feminist criticism. The contemporary British Caribbean writer Jean Rhys' adaptation of Charlotte Bronte's canonical novel *Jane Eyre* and the contemporary Black Canadian playwright Djanet Sears's adaptation of William Shakespeare's *Othello* in her drama play *Harlem Duet* require a special treatment, as both rewrites undertake the form of prequel adaptation—a specific type of adaptation that intends to tell the previous story of the characters in the source text.

The contemporary British writer Jean Rhys' postcolonial feminist novel, *Wide Sargasso Sea*, can be considered among the prominent works of the contemporary British narrative. The novel is usually studied as a rewrite of Charlotte Brontë's *Jane Eyre*, through which Rhys freely enters the mainstream discourses. However, the strength of Rhys' novel lies more in its challenge to the boundaries of conventional subject matter and form on both narrative and authorial layers. In other words, the conventional discourses of nineteenth-century Europe are subverted thematically in the novel,

CHAPTER 4

while one of the canonical texts of English literature is being revised. This paper examines Rhys' work in relation to the postcolonial theorist Homi K. Bhabha's conception of "the third space" (1994: 41), in terms of both content and structure, while it reads the novel's revision of Brontë's *Jane Eyre* within this conciliatory context. In her revolutionary novel, Jean Rhys revisits the lunatic Mrs. Rochester of Charlotte Brontë's *Jane Eyre*, who lives in the attic. Coming from a white Caribbean (Creole) background herself, Rhys notes in her foreword that what she intended to do is "to give her a life" (1999) and thus situates the former Mrs. Rochester, the Creole Antoinette, at the centre of her novel. Giving Antoinette an individual voice and a different perspective, Rhys presents what Brontë's novel leaves out. Rhys' novel is very innovative for its critical treatment of colonial and patriarchal order as well as for its status as a loose adaptation.

The novel announces its adaptive strategy in continuously juxtaposing narrative voices and perspectives provided by Antoinette Bertha and Edward Rochester. To exemplify, in Part I, the narrator/character, young Antoinette, tells the reader about her childhood and early youth. Part 2 starts with Edward Rochester's narration of his wife, Antoinette Bertha Mason, and their life in her native land. Narrated by Antoinette Bertha in psychosis, Part 3 echoes the chapter of *Jane Eyre* in which Bertha tries to set the house on fire. From the very beginning, *Wide Sargasso Sea* announces its subversion of patriarchy, orienting the reader with a female household, including the heroine Antoinette, her mother Annette, Annette's sister, Cora, and their assistants Christophine and Tia. The only exception, Antoinette's brother Pierre, is depicted as a submissive and helpless figure. Another male figure introduced to the household is Mr. Mason, who marries Annette and obeys their rules out of his strong love for Annette.

Part 2, which starts with a shift in the narrative voice from Antoinette's to her husband's, reflects a patriarchal perspective. Edward's narration focuses on his perception of Antoinette's native land, where he feels thoroughly isolated. He not only feels distanced from the island, which is a female territory, but also detests the land's location in savage nature. Because the island is thoroughly unlike Edward's hometown, London, and Edward fails in his attempts to adapt to the new order, he acts as an outsider. The island is "too much of everything" as Edward puts forth, while London is consistently "civil" (1999: 95–97). Similarly, Edward is obsessed with the presence of a secret in the land and tries to uncover that. Edward's attitude towards conquering and demystifying the land is very reminiscent of the orientalist discourses, which suggest the Orient is only something to explore from the perspective of the Occident. In this respect, Edward owns the colonialist gaze in his treatment of the land and its people, considering them as both enjoyable and scary, mysterious and primitive. Edward's following words about the land reveal his Orientalism: "It was a beautiful place-wild, untouched, with an alien, disturbing, secret loveliness. And it keeps its secret". In other words, like all colonisers, Edward finds joy in asserting his superior position by intending to explore his Other, which he calls the "god-forsaken-land" (Rhys 1999: 96).

The binary opposites, such as nature versus culture, the matriarchal versus the patriarchal, the coloniser versus the colonised, are inevitably reflected in his narration through Edward's limited understanding of the land, which, similar to Antoinette and the other female inhabitants, is his Other. Antoinette and the land gradually become one in his narration, and Edward becomes gradually distanced from his wife: "She held up the skirt of her riding habit and ran across the Street. I watched her critically. She wore a tricorne hat which became her. At least it shadowed her eyes which are too large and can be disconcerting. She never blinks at all she seems to me. Long, sad, dark, alien eyes. Creole of pure English descent she may be, but they are not English or European either..." (Rhys 1999: 39).

Edward Rochester's above-quoted lines convey a strong feeling of superiority over Antoinette. As he observes Antoinette from a "critical" point of view, he examines Antoinette's physical appearance in implied comparison with those of English and European women. In this respect, Edward's perspective can be read as both patriarchal and colonialist. Edward's relations with other female inhabitants of the land also involve patriarchal and colonial perspectives. To specify, he views both Christophine and Amelia as a part of the mysterious atmosphere, usually commodifying them and often reflecting them with both condemnation and fear. For instance, Edward attempts to have sexual intercourse with Amelia while he describes her physical appearance quite stereotypically, as "dark skin, thick lips" in Part II (1999: 87). Similarly, Edward frequently owns a critical perspective towards Christophine and often complains to Antoinette about Christophine's non-standard use of English. In other words, Edward usually places England and his English identity as the "norm" or the "standard", evaluating Others only on such a comparative scale.

Associating "realness" and "truth" with his hometown, Edward can only define the reality in Antoinette's land in relation to "magic" and truth through "dream": "I was certain that everything I imagined to be truth was false. Only the magic and dream are true-the rest is a lie" (1999: 101). According to Said, the encounter with the Other may also reveal a sense of fear (1978). Edward is afraid of the power of nature these female characters entail: "Then she cursed me comprehensively, my eyes, my mouth, every member of my body..." (1999: 89). Edward's choice of such a strong word as "curse" parallels his suspicious theories about the presence of magic in the land. In one of his conversations with Antoinette, Edward asks her if she was afraid of Christophine, which implies his own fear. In these words, Edward both addresses Christophine as his Other and recognises her different power.

"In-betweenness" or "hybridity", which Homi K. Bhabha relates to the colonial encounter in his celebrated work *The Location of Culture* (1994), is probably the most problematic stage of the colonial discourse since it induces William Edward Burghardt Du Bois's conception of "double conscious-ness" (1994: 2), besides double vision and double voice. Antoinette, being a second-generation Martinique and British girl, announces her hybridity through her in-between perspective. She experiences a total non-belonging, which is reflected onto her narration: "I never looked at any strange negro. They hated us. They called us white cockroaches" (Rhys 1999: 13). She was excluded by both white and Black communities, which probably led to her ambiguous self-conception: "Real white people, they got gold Money. They didn't look at us, nobody see them come near us. Old time white people nothing but white nigger now, and black nigger beter than white nigger" (1999: 14). Antoinette's ambivalent identity is further explored through the looking glass imagery throughout the novel. The looking glass can be taken as a signifier of Antoinette's location of self through the Other. As Du Bois suggests, the coloured self often internalises the Other's perspective directed to himself/herself. What Du Bois calls "double consciousness" or "internalized otherness" is exhibited through young Antoinette's two reflections on the coloured Tia and the English girl, Helene, respectively: "As I ran, I thought I will live with Tia and be like her. Not to leave Coulibri. Not to go. Not. When I was close I saw the jagged stone in her hand but I did not see her throw it. I did not feel it either, only something wet, running down my face. I looked at her and I saw her face crumple up as she began to cry. We stared at each other, blood on my face, tears on her. It was as if I saw myself. Like in a looking glass" (Rhys 1999: 27). On the one hand lies Antoinette's identification with her coloured friend, Tia, while on the other hand lies her opposite identification with the blonde Helen:

> "Please Helene, tell me how you do your hair, please when I grow up I want mine to look like yours."
> "It's very easy. You comb it upwards, like this and then push it a little forward, like that, and then you pin it here and here. Never too many pins."
> "Yes, but Helene, mine does not look like yours, whatever I do" (1999: 32).

In her above conversation with her roommate, Helene, Antoinette mentions the absence of any looking glass in their dorm. Much later in the novel, in psychosis, Antoinette notes her lack of any looking glass in her room. The recurrent references to the looking glass, while it is not physically present, imply Antoinette's problematic location of self. Her obsession with Helene's style of hair reflects her intention to comprehend the physical difference between the English and the Creole, in front of the looking glass. Encountering both sides of the binary opposite Black and white in her mirror image, Antoinette hardly reconciles with her ambiguous self-reflection.

In its three parts, *Wide Sargasso Sea* successfully incorporates different voices and juxtaposes alternative perspectives of young Antoinette, Edward and Antoinette Bertha Rochester, respectively. Introducing a sense of duality throughout the narrative, one being female and colonised, the other being male and coloniser, the text consistently foregrounds an in-between situation. In this respect, the text adheres to Homi K. Bhabha's suggestion of "hybridity", "ambivalence" and "multivocality" as a means of destabilising the binary opposites (1994: 40–43). Transcribing the whole experience in a hybrid phase where the Creole woman and the English man can coexist, the text itself signifies Homi K. Bhabha's notion of "the third space" where colonial encounter becomes "negotiable". While Antoinette and Edward's stories refute one another, the duality and relativity of their perspectives become central to the readers' attention. While the subjectivity of truth, multiplicity of voice and plurality of perspective are celebrated, the text's revolution is announced by Antoinette as "There is always the other side, always" and reflects on Rhys' motivation in writing the novel: I've read and re-read "Jane Eyre", of course, and I am sure that the character must be "built-up". I wrote you about that. The Creole in Charlotte Brontë's novel is a lay figure-repulsive, which does not matter, and not once alive, which does. She's necessary to the plot, but she always shrieks, howls, laughs horribly, attacks all and sundry off-stage. She must be at least plausible with a past, the reason why Mr. Rochester treats her so abominably and feels justified, the reason why he thinks she is mad and why, of course, she goes mad, even the reason she tries to set everything on fire, and eventually succeeds. I don't see how Charlotte Brontë's mad woman could possibly convey all this. It might be done, but it would not be convincing. At least I doubt it. Another "I" must talk, two others perhaps. Then the Creole's "I" will come to life.

The above lines, quoted from Rhys's letter to Selma Vaz Dias, show that the writer intends to give the lunatic, Creole Mrs. Rochester in the attic a life as well as a distinct voice. As a Creole herself, Rhys also makes it clear that the Creole subject embodies two "I"s, as a reflection of the hybrid identity. While Brontë's novel presents a pure English heroine speaking with a single voice and vision, Rhys revises the canonical *Jane Eyre* with her innovative incorporation of double voice and double vision throughout *Wide Sargasso Sea* and writes her back into the novel. In this respect, Rhys' revision reinforces Adrienne Rich's understanding of the term as "the act of looking back, of seeing with fresh eyes, of entering an old text from a new critical direction..." (1992: 369). Responding to Rich's following lines, "We have to know the writing of the past and know it differently than we have ever known it; not to pass on a tradition but to break its hold over us" (1999: 362), Rhys' text resists the oppressive traditions of the past.

The adaptive choice in the narrative structure and devices demonstrates Rhys's novel's revolution in subverting the dominant discourses of patriarchy and colonialism. The novel, which opens with a first-person narrator, Antoinette, focalising her own childhood, hardly provokes any trust in the reader. Since the narration is retrospective, the childish gaze is often overshadowed by the intrusions of Antoinette as an adult narrator. Furthermore, there are transitions between diegetic and extradiegetic narration, blurring the omniscience of the perspective. For instance, the novel employs two narrative voices throughout the narration. The first part being Antoinette's, the second one being Edward's, with transitions from his perspective to hers, and the third part being Antoinette's, the text does not follow any standard form. Furthermore, the linear progression of the novel is frequently blocked through the juxtaposition of opposing views and different visions by Antoinette and Edward.

The text is also hybrid, on the authorial layer, owing to its conscious intertextual dialogues with Brontë's novel. While the major characters are those of the nineteenth-century English writer Charlotte Brontë's, the story and discourse are provided by the contemporary Creole writer Jean Rhys. As Rhys centralises Antoinette Bertha Mason Rochester in her novel, her adaptive strategy is revealed in sparing her heroine two-thirds of the narration. In other words, reversing the power structures in Brontë's text, namely the perspective and the narrative voice, Rhys privileges the formerly disadvantaged Antoinette.

Rhys' adaptive strategies in rewriting *Jane Eyre* remind the postcolonial reader of Homi K. Bhabha's above-explained understanding of "hybridity" and "third space", the neutral grounds of which provide a chance to negotiate the colonial Others. Actually, Rhys does not choose to present Antoinette as Jane's Other, locating her heroine between the coloured Tia and the English Helene. Most of the criticism on *Wide Sargasso Sea* does not focus on the significance of Helene for the novel. Helene is not only Antoinette's childhood friend from the dormitory but also a metaphor for the English half of Antoinette's identity. However, Helene, whom Antoinette envies for her straight hair, is more functional than other similar metaphors of Englishness, such as the portrait of the blonde "Miller's Daughter" or Antoinette's second name, Bertha. Helene can also be read as a reflection of Helene Burns in *Jane Eyre*, who is depicted as Jane's dorm friend and her childhood idol, several years older than herself. In this respect, the presence of Helene in both Antoinette and Jane's childhood does not set them further apart but brings them closer. Similar to Antoinette, who envies Helene's hair, Jane envies Helene's beauty, being not very beautiful herself. As children, both Antoinette and Jane are raised half in dormitories and half by nannies, Christophine and Bessie. They have similar unpleasant memories of their male relatives, Sandi Cosway and John Reed. Finally, they marry the same Mr. Rochester.

The postcolonial feminist theorist Gayatri C. Spivak argues that Antoinette has to become "the fictive Other" inevitably, so that Jane Eyre can become "the heroine" of the English feminist canon. Similarly, Serena Reavis considers the encounter between Jane and Antoinette as a "struggle", viewing both characters as "subaltern" (2014). On the other hand, she reads the dialogue between *Jane Eyre* and *Wide Sargasso Sea* also as a "third space", however meant "for the enunciation of the other", although she realises the relevance of Bhabhian "ambivalence" in this context. However, Antoinette is both similar to and different from Jane since hybridity implies "being both one and the Other" while being "neither one nor the Other" at the same time. Jane represents one half of Antoinette's identity, English, and the other half, Caribbean, is what Jane is not. Therefore, Antoinette's hybrid self, her Creole identity, cannot be considered the exact opposite of Jane Eyre, just like *Wide Sargasso Sea* intends not to deconstruct but rather to revise *Jane Eyre*. Spivak also notes that Rhys articulates the situation of Creole/ white Caribbean and fails to introduce an insight into the black Caribbean (1988: 844). Spivak remarks that Christophine is depicted as a strong black female figure; she considers her presence in the text as comparatively secondary to other female characters (1988: 845, 846). The following words by Christophine justify Rhys' strategy to offer her as a coloured female figure of alternative wisdom: "Read and write I don't know. Other things I know" (Rhys 1999: 97). Christophine is obviously present in the novel with the other things she knows and consciously prefers over the conventional understanding of wisdom, intellectuality. To exemplify, Christophine chooses not to alter her English despite Edward's criticism and affectively asserts her power through obeah, cooking, singing and story-telling. However, as Spivak notes, Rhys does not locate the black Caribbean Christophine at the centre of her text, because as she mentions in her letter to Selma Van Dias, Rhys intends to give the Creole a life. As she chooses the genre of adaptation, Rhys wishes to build on Brontë's text instead of writing a thoroughly new text. In other words, *Wide Sargasso Sea* can be considered as a "repetition without replication" or a "re-interpretation" (Hutcheon 2006), deliberately distancing itself from its source text.

In this adaptive process, Rhys's text intends to deconstruct or subvert the conventional power structures, avoiding any reversal. Choosing her heroine as Antoinette but not as Christophine, and adopting the structure of adaptation which is, as Julie Sanders defines it, a "hybridized form" (2006), Rhys offers a reconciliatory attitude in the above-mentioned Bhabhian sense. Given this context, her choice to end her novel at the point where

Jane Eyre starts, which Spivak also criticises, rather shows the consistency of her adaptive strategy.

Rhys's novel challenges the conventional techniques of narration and offers a new discourse. The juxtaposition of alternative narrative voices and different perspectives, as well as the nonlinear progression of narration, point out a noteworthy distance from the nineteenth-century English context. The letters from Cosway, which block the validity of narrations or Antoinette and Edward's stories refuting one another, contribute to the relative presentation of truth and structurally enable *Wide Sargasso Sea* to offer a social critique on the conventional structures of power, namely patriarchy and colonialism. Decentralising the conventional English character Jane Eyre and relocating Antoinette and announcing her with her full name "Antoinette Bertha Mason Rochester", Rhys emphasises the hybrid identity of her Creole heroine.

Renaming the doubly Other'ed "lunatic" Creole in the attic and giving her a voice, Rhys decolonises Antoinette's spirit, which may be supported by Antoinette's note at the lunatic stage, in Part 3, on her soul freely traveling into their world (1966). While on a thematic level, Rhys gradually develops the story into the colonial encounter between Jane and Antoinette, she technically challenges the binary opposites defining them as self and the Other. Rhys' adaptive strategy, in accordance with Bhabhian understanding of "third space", uses the textual potential of fiction in offering a neutral space where all reflections of difference can "negotiate" (Bhabha 1994). That "third space" can here be addressed as the text's adaptive form itself, where the past and the present, the canonised and the noncanonised, can coexist.

In her awarded play, *Harlem Duet*, Djanet Sears also follows the method of prequel adaptation in revisiting William Shakespeare's *Othello* in a black Canadian context. Djanet Sears is a black Canadian playwright, actor, director and drama teacher, who was nationally awarded for her drama play *Harlem Duet* several times. Sears provides Othello with a background before his marriage to Desdemona, whom Sears calls Mona, shortly, and briefly accommodates in one scene. Sears's play dramatises Othello's choice to marry a white woman, after a love affair with a black woman called Billy in Harlem City. In *Harlem Duet*, Othello is represented as an ambitious black subject with a strong intellectual background. His urge to become visible in American society motivates Othello to start a romantic relationship with his white colleague. That he gets promoted shortly after his marriage to Mona and becomes the coordinator of the department in Cyprus explicitly indicates a correlation. Reminiscent of Shakespeare's antagonist Iago by the name as well as the rivalry in-between, Chris Yago stands among the white scholars Othello is obsessed with the idea of impressing.

Reflecting its resistance to colonial and patriarchal signifiers of *Othello*, Sears's play reminds the audience of the following lines by Othello, even before the Prologue:

> ….. That handkerchief,
> Did a Egyptian to my mother give.
> She was a charmer…
> There's magic in the web of it.
> A sibyl… in her prophetic fury sewed the work (Shakespeare 1988, Act III, Scene 4).

In Shakespearean text, the handkerchief stands as a metaphor for Othello's African background, as it originally belongs to a North African woman and passes on to Othello's African mother as a gift. Desdemona's loss of the handkerchief, which Othello gives her as a wedding gift, pointing out its relation to his mother, reinforces the fall of Othello's female bondage. The story of the handkerchief also implies the betrayal within womanhood since Emilia collaborates with Iago in its passing to Cassio, and Bianca instrumentally takes her part. Reinforcing her postcolonial feminist context in adapting *Othello*, Djanet Sears makes sure to revisit the handkerchief several times in her play. In Act I, which opens in 1928 Harlem, Billie reminds Othello of his gift to her, his mother's handkerchief. Given the context of Harlem and its historical significance owing to the black cultural movement called Harlem Renaissance in the 1920s, the handkerchief is recalled in a nostalgic tone, as a means of celebration of African heritage.

Another noteworthy reference to the handkerchief comes in the middle of Billie and Othello's dispute, as Billie asks Othello if he loves Mona and whether Mona is white. Billie tries to give the handkerchief back to Othello, who initially refuses to take it. Given this context, Sears makes a very effective use of the flashback technique in staging the scene in which Othello gave Billie the handkerchief, back in 1860 Harlem, in Act I, Scene 2. The handkerchief is also revisited within the context of revenge as Billie uses the handkerchief as a tool for her black spell targeting Othello and Mona's relationship. Pouring a few drops of blood from her miscarriage of Othello's child, which she had kept frozen for years, onto the handkerchief, Billie passes it to Othello. When Othello again refuses to take the handkerchief, Billie implies his indifferent attitude towards his own ancestry by interpreting Othello's attitude as a sign of his disinterest in his mother's handkerchief.

Another innovation is in incorporating Canada as one of the characters in the play. Canada, Billie's father, who in Act II comes to visit Billie, displays a very confronting attitude despite the power Dynamics in the house. Billie and Othello's common yearning for living in Canada, where "freedom came" (2000: 294) before the States, also situates Canada as a potential address for an optimistic sense of the future. Within the time span of the drama play, the States goes through two important historical periods, such as Emancipation and Harlem Renaissance, both of which imply difficult times for people of colour. As his following lines indicate, even Othello, who does not consider himself "minority" and calls himself "an American" (2000: 305), suffers from "ambivalent identity" as Du Bois puts it forth (1994: 3–5): "If you don't hear my educated English, if you don't understand that I am a middle class educated man. I mean what does Africa have to do with me. We struttin' around professing some imaginary connection for a land we don't know. Never seen. Never gonna see" (2000: 305). Billie's critical gaze on Othello's internalised Otherness reminds one of Du Bois's conception of "double consciousness", which the theorist defines as "the sense of always looking at oneself through the eyes of the other" (1994: 2).

In Mat Buntin's interview, Djanet Sears notes that one of her inspirations for the project has been the blackface image, which caught her attention negatively as she watched Laurence Olivier's performance of *Othello* (web). Providing a reverse minstrel show has probably been the strongest underlying motivation to undertake the adaptive method of prequel. In one of their conversations, Billie corrects Othello, who calls himself "an actor" as "a black minstrel" (2000: 312). Furthermore, Billie finds a mask among Othello's properties and passes it to the landlady to keep it. In another scene where Othello visits Billie to take his packed boxes, he steps on a piece of the broken mask and puts it on the mantel (2000: 304). It is noteworthy that each and every one of these scenes on the mask is accompanied by crucial discussions on racial identity. In this respect, the mask signifies Othello's role in the white society, which he chooses over the Harlem tradition. "Storytelling" and "rememory" are also among the traditional black techniques Sears incorporates into *Harlem*

Duet. Its ontological status as a prequel to Shakespeare's *Othello* implies that *Harlem Duet* intends to tell Othello's previous story as surrounded by Billie and Harlem culture. The convention of rememory also gets reinforced with effective use of flashback, evoking a sense that the present moment and space are caught by past memories. Margaret Jane Kidnie reads Sears's adaptation as a means of "exorcizing the past" and haunting "a theatrical ghost" through a recognition of black traditions (2000: 71). In Buntin's interview, Djanet Sears adds that "… when adapting Shakespeare, we are trying to break away from our foundational mythologies by revisioning them and in doing so, we create a new covenant, a new testament" (web). Sears provides Othello and Billie in a conversation as they share their books by Shakespeare, as well as those on African mythology. With extended intertextual techniques, Sears makes Billie address Othello within Shakespearean recognition. The lines "White wisdom from the mouth of a mythical Negro" (2000: 304), for instance, imply the canonical position of Shakespeare's Othello.

Sears's accommodation of black man and black woman relations is reminiscent of bell hooks' suggestion of "chain of oppression" where black woman is situated at the very bottom scale (hooks 2006: 16), while Billie's question "Ain't I A Woman" reflects on both bell hooks and Sojourner Truth's titles. Djanet Sears reverses the conventional attitude towards black women and dethrones Desdemona from the text by leaving her reduced to an off-stage voice, as metaphorically projected onto her abbreviated name, Mona. In *Harlem Duet*, Djanet Sears offers a strong black feminist Canadian appropriation of Shakespeare's *Othello*. The adaptive method of prequel enables her to tell the previous story of Othello before his marriage to Desdemona. In this respect, the play dethrones both Othello and Desdemona from the story and centralises the black woman Billie as surrounded by the context of Harlem.

Given this context, Jean Rhys and Djanet Sears's prequel adaptations resist the colonial and patriarchal markers embedded in the canonical texts *Jane Eyre* by Charlotte Bronte and *Othello* by William Shakespeare. Claiming that they are telling the previous stories surrounding the central male characters of Bronte and Shakespeare's texts, namely Edward Rochester and Othello, *Wide Sargasso Sea* and *Harlem Duet* strongly resist their canonical power, by offering alternatives to established stories and by reversing the conventional sense of chronology. Giving voices to two coloured women, Antoinette and

Billie, the texts announce their target contexts as more central, even with their choices of titles, *Wide Sargasso Sea* and *Harlem Duet*, respectively.

References

Bhabha, Homi K., *The Location of Culture*. London, New York: Routledge, 1994.

Brontë, Charlotte, *Jane Eyre*. London: Penguin P, 1994 (1847).

Buntin, Mat. "Interview With Djanet Sears". March 2004. www.canadianshakespeares.ca/i_dsears.cfm.10.10.2016. (web)

Du Bois, William Edward Burghardt, *The Souls of Black Folk*. New York: Dover P, 1994 (1903).

hooks, bell. *Feminist Theory: From Margin to Center*. London: Pluto P, 2000.

Hutcheon, Linda, *A Theory of Adaptation*. New York, London: Routledge P, 2006.

Kidnie, Margaret Jane. *Shakespeare and The Problem of Adaptation*. London. New York: Routledge P, 2009.

Reavis, Serena, "'Myself Yet Not Quite Myself'. Jane Eyre, Wide Sargasso Sea and A Third Space of Enunciation". http://libres.uncg.edu/ir/uncg/f/umi-uncg- 1088.pdf / 30.07.2014. (web).

Rhys, Jean, *Wide Sargasso Sea*. Judith L. Raiskin Ed. New York: London and Norton Company P, 1999 (1966).

Rich, Adrienne, "When We Dead Awaken". *Feminisms: A Reader*. Ed. Maggie Humm. Hemel Hempstead: Harvester Wheatsheaf, 1992.

Said, Edward, *Orientalism*. Harmondsworth: Penguin P, 1995 (1978).

Sanders, Julie, *Adaptation and Appropriation*. London, New York: Routledge, 2006.

Sears, Djanet. "Harlem Duet". *Adaptations of Shakespeare*. Eds. Daniel Fischlin and Mark Fortier. New York: Routledge, 2000.

Shakespeare, William. Tragedies: *The Tragedy of Othello, The Moor of Venice*. London: Marshall Cavendish, 1988.

Spivak, Gayatri C., "Three Women's Texts and A Critique of Imperialism". *Literary Theory: An Anthology*. Ed. Julie Rivkin and Michael Ryan. Malden, MA: Blackwell P, 1988. 838–851.

Intertextual, Intergeneric Reflections and the Posthuman: Sylvia Plath's *Ariel* and Ntozake Shange's *From Okra to Green*

Posthumanist understanding, which criticises the hierarchical positioning of man over the environment inevitably reflects on formations of and relations between textualities, while classical definitions of art situates in relation to nature. Involving central intertextual and intergeneric dialogues, Contemporary American poets Sylvia Plath and Ntozake Shange's poetry responds to the everlasting question of man in relation to the environment.

> First follow NATURE and your judgement frame,
> By its just standard, which is still the same.
> Those rules of old, discover'd, not devised,
> Are Nature still, but Nature methodized;
> Nature, like Liberty, is but restrain'd
> By the same laws which first herself ordain'd (Pope L. 1–6).

Alexander Pope's above-quoted lines beautifully address man's instinctual reflection and projection of nature as an inevitable destination towards artistic production. From the Augustan Period onwards, it has been a recurrent point of reference that a good literary work, structurally, reflects patterns of nature. Nature has also been thematically accommodated in literature, not only as literature on environment but also as nature embedded in the depiction/representation of the central character whose thoughts and decisions are overrun by emotions. Given this context, narrative and diegetic genres of contemporary literature appeal more to scholarly interest as compared to the genre of poetry. Although ecopoetic specifically deals with nature and poetry, it does not fully accommodate intergeneric poems. Literature survey on environmental poetry with certain narrative and dramatic qualities, involving those of Sylvia

Plath and Ntozake Shange, demonstrates a limited number of studies on their intergeneric structures despite the scholarly interest Plath and Shange have commonly received as two inspiring contemporary American women poets. Guided by Rosi Braidotti's theories on posthumanism, this study looks into Sylvia Plath and Ntozake Shange's intertextual and intergeneric dialogues with myths as reflections of "a time when the world was still young and people had a connection with the earth" (Hamilton 1999: 13) in relation to the two women poets' parallel journeys at the crossroads between private and public, individual and collective, writerly and anonymous, bodily and spiritual, and stable and unstable experiences. This study contends to highlight that Sylvia Plath and Ntozake Shange's environmental poems not only thematically project their philosophical stances but also structurally resist mainstream understandings and reflections. In this respect, this study offers a comparative perspective in looking into Plath's and Shange's innovative poetry collections together.

Published in 1965, in the rich poetry collection with the same title, Sylvia Plath's poem "Ariel" has been well-studied for its intriguing content and experimental form. However, its innovation lies in its dialogue with mythology as well as Rosi Braidotti's recently rising conception of "nomadic subject" (2014). The poem embodies passion, ambiguity and disintegration by dwelling on the horseback rider's physical and spiritual journey with a horse named Ariel. "Ariel" accommodates the poetic persona's search for identity in its ambivalent presentation of the horse and the horseback rider as constantly shifting subjects and/or objects while employing an ambiguous structure through a juxtaposition of another binary opposite, namely run-on and/or fragmentation.

While biographical sources indicate that Ariel was the name of the horse Plath used to ride in Devon, the choice of the name Ariel for the horse, as well as the title, implies two possible intertextual dialogues with the canon: Lion-headed deity with power over the Earth as Greek mythology puts it and Shakespeare's fairy in *Tempest*, who is obliged to serve Prospero. Both texts foreground Ariel as a shape-shifting entity, reminiscent of that of Plath. At times, the poetic persona is about to lose her control over the horse. The poetic persona is very careful about keeping her balance, especially as they passes through a pastoral landscape. While references to nature imply an orderly, coherent structure, the passion of the ride contradicts this mood by introducing chaos to these peaceful surroundings. The fragmented structure of the poem accompanies the passionate mood portrayed. The transformation of pastoral qualities to lyric ones also supports the parallelism between chaos and order. The stable, peaceful associations concerning nature are connoted as a dynamic one when the lyrical passion is added to it. In this respect, the mood of the poetic persona may be associated with the transition between a peaceful mood and a passionate one. In addition, the pastoral journey is accompanied by a deeper journey that the persona goes through, the quest.

Ambiguity is another crucial element, finding its voice in the central conflict of the poetic persona. The poetic persona's pragmatic intentions on the body of the horse are very explicit in the following choice of words, which point out Ariel as the object of the riding journey: "God's lioness", "nigger-eye". In other words, these two references imply that at the beginning, the poetic persona views the horse as a mysterious substance, evoking her curiosity. However, "statis in darkness" and "substanceless blue skies" introduce the forthcoming dilemma the poetic persona experiences in her journey within nature. That the same sky is both "dark" and "blue" in her depiction indicates her subjective associations of nature with both danger and mystery. The subject and object reflections are presented in such an interchangeable context and structure that nature becomes both the threatening subject and the object to be grasped and solved. Similarly, the horse Ariel plays an instrumental role in conveying this central ambiguity through the identification of the bodies of the rider and the horse:

Black sweet blood mouthfuls,
Shadows.
Something else
Hauls me through the air-
Thighs, hair;
Flakes from my heels. (Plath, 1981: L 13-18)

As this quote clearly demonstrates, the poetic persona becomes controlled by an alternative body. Who is the riding subject and who is the ridden object remains an unsolved mystery throughout the poem, which, through the riding process, offers a space where the two bodies "encounter" and "reconcile", reminiscent of Homi K. Bhabha's conception of "third space", where the coloniser and the colonised can potentially negotiate (1994: 218). The references to "thighs" and "hair", in this respect, stand for the encounter of two thighs and two hair in the "third space" that the riding process itself accommodates.

The notion of disintegration is the most foregrounding dilemma, which accounts for the motivation of the journey, in turn, the quest. The poetic persona, as the rider needs to grasp the "sloping curve of the horse's neck" so as not to fall. That she cannot hold Ariel's neck, she cannot keep her balance, implies that her body depends on Ariel's body in this process. In terms of her mind, the situation is quite similar since her vision and gaze are thoroughly directed by the angle the horse leads to. In other words, the subject and the object change positions, gradually, since they are being continuously juxtaposed. In the poem, the disintegration of body and mind or soul serves as one required stage before the later unification of the two bodies as well as minds or souls.

With references to "foam"ing and "melt"ing, the eighth and the ninth stanzas display a disintegration of her body and soul. She and the horse become a single arrow shot into the eyes of the sun. They dissolve there as dew dissolves in morning light:

> And now I
> Foam to wheat, a glitter of seas.
> The child's cry
>
> Melts in the Wall
> And I
> Am the arrow,
>
> The dew that flies
> Suicidal, at one with the drive
> Into the red
>
> Eye, the cauldron of morning (Plath 1981: L. 22–31).

She identifies herself with "the dew" in terms of their suicidal flight. This suicide further signifies the disintegration of body and soul as well as the poetic persona's bodily sacrifice for unison with that of the horse. Similarly,

"I" becomes a collective one, her voice grows more decisive despite her unsure, weaker state in the middle of the poem. While "I" is now a collective one, the "eye" is transformed into a more objective state. This "eye", being "the cauldron of morning", is that of the sun, which is the gaze of nature. Therefore, these last lines announce a rebirth of the persona to nature, from Ariel's body. In this respect, the poetic persona's unification with nature through Ariel assigns Ariel the role of an evoker and reinforces Rosi Braidotti's contemporary conception of "nomadic subject's" "becoming" process, which deconstructs the earlier defined binary opposites. As Braidotti theorises on the two poles's potential sameness, her major argument dwells on the point of a long neglected "connection" (2014: 170–175).

The form of the poem adheres to its content since it reflects passion, ambiguity, and disintegration all at once, before the last stage of "connection" and unification. The fragmentation and ambiguous referentiality in language contribute to the mood of the content. The strong voice gradually gets weaker as its complete lines turn into hyphenated sentences. The unconscious "I" that fails to locate in a body finds another body through riding. Hence, the last lines are assertive in tone, consisting of full statements. While the hyphenations convey both passion and disintegration, the ambiguity of references contributes to the mysterious tone of the poem. Ten three-line stanzas and a final single line for closure incorporate action in such a way that the subject and the object become blurred. The telegraphic meter, through which the transition between the lines is made possible problematises the referentiality. As one image breaks off, another begins while the subject and the object become merged. As the poetic persona finally "unpeels" on a metaphorical layer, she quits her individual existence, leaving all her cultural donations behind. At the end, she feels liberated, which is reinforced through references to nature in possessing her and transforming her into a collectivity. Given this context, Sylvia Plath's poem calls the contemporary reader for rethinking the riding subject's ever-transforming journey under the light of Rosi Braidotti's conception of "nomadic subject" (2014: 170–175), both thematically and structurally. While the poetic persona dissolves into the universe, in turn collectivity, "unpeel"ing her personal connotations, there is a note on the sun above.

When Ntozake Shange's "From Okra to Greens" was published in 1984 for stage purposes, the collection of poetry was highly criticised by a number of scholars, including Neal A. Lester, for not having an inner coherence (224), in response to which Shange notes that she is a poet, not a dramatist. The writing of the poetry collection coincides with Ntozake Shange's process of medication under "bipolar" mood, which requires a closer look for its parallelism with Plath's emotional state. Reminiscent of black vernacular tradition, Shange depicts Okra, prototypically, as any black woman and Greens as the black male companion. For instance, the first time they meet, the note on Okra "the woman who don't stand up straight aint never stto up straight" (1) implies a crooked, introvert figure. As Okra's attempts to stand up end in failure and she gets even more curled over at the end, the poetic persona shares what lies beneath this posture:

> Wasn't just she cdnt stand up straight/she cdn
> Hardly keep somebody else's body outta hers
> &since everybody cd see/immediately
> This child always bends over
> Always twists round herself to
> Keep from standing up (Shange 1984: 3)

The use of the word "child" in the above-quoted depiction strongly conveys the need for protection as the major reason for her inability to stand straight. Also, reading these lines as signs of identification with nature, Neal A. Lester traces this motive to a collective wish to crawl back to the earth, even to go back to the mother's womb (1995: 259). While Okra encounters the male figure, Green, in a closet, the poetic persona intoduces him as who "...didnt know what a stood/up straight man felt like" (1984: 3) and further notes the role of culture in this division: "they curled round/nobody cd tell anymore/ what to get outta the way of&they never spoke/of their condition" (1984: 3). These references to their bodily encounter involve sexual connotations, indirectly presented. Owning the black female gaze in her approach towards Greens, Okra recalls stories told to her by her grandma and assures, "that's why I like GREENS/I know how to cook 'em" (1984: 5). Parallel to the use of black vernacular in language, the above-quoted lines imply rootedness in relation to memories of black female ancestry and their conceptions of black man as something to manipulate. As Okra and Greens walk at the heart of nature, they are accompanied by the rhythms of blues. The poem builds on the distinction between nature versus culture, also by embodying a sociopolitical discussion on language. To the question Okra asks on what language the song is in, Greens responds that it is simply a way to ask her to give him her tongue (1984: 10). This conversation deconstructs the sociopolitical aspect of language by offering an alternative in body language instead. This interplay between literal and metaphorical senses of the word "tongue" implies an intertextual engagement with the West African myth of the trickster, signifying monkey. In the African vernacular tradition, the monkey plays an intricate game with the lion through their mutual friend, elephant. Using the elephant instrumentally for signification, the monkey constantly signifies on the simplest things. Unable to decode the monkey's complicated figurative level of speech and taking his words on the literal level, the lion gets eventually duped. Drawing on the myth, Henry Louis Gates suggests that the signifying monkey breaks the authority of the lion, the king, through ongoing mimicry and further traces the black tradition of writing to this myth of the trickster, which epitomises the manner in which the tradition undertakes continuous signification (1988: 56–58). In signifying on Okra's wording, Green's act resembles that of the trickster figure, the signifying monkey. In this respect, Ntozake Shange's poem reinforces Gates's suggestion of "signifying on" (1988: 56) as a common pattern and an embedded intertextual dialogue within the black literary tradition itself.

The below quote from "The Signifying Monkey" also implies a structural similarity:

> The Monkey and the Lion
> Got to talking one dsay.
> Monkey looked down and said. Lion,
> I hear you's a king in every way.
> But I know somebody
> Who do not think that it is true-
> He told me he could whip
> The living daylights out of you.

Not only does the twisting image of the bending over child allude to the circular patterns in the signifying monkey's speech, but the story-telling mood in Shange's poem also echoes the black vernacular tradition.

On the other hand, "From Okra to Greens", conventionally, locates man on the side of culture as Okra's reference to the land as "father land" (1984: 24) and to black man as "kindergarten teachers" (1984: 22), implies. On the contrary, women are stereotypically depicted in relation to nature. Given this context, Green's final betrayal of Okra reinforces the black feminist theorists, bell hooks' conception of "chain of oppression" as a process of oppression where black women, placed at the bottom of the step-ladder, inevitably suffer the most (1989: 4–13). As Green leaves Okra towards the end of the poem, Okra's final depiction under the sun echoes the same image of a curled woman again. This return to her past state, both supports the traditional association of women with nature; "When you disappeared/a tremendous silence shook/ My body till my bones split/I hadta grab my sinews/From the mouths of bats" (1984: 19) and highlights the instrumental role Greens had in Okra's life, in accompanying her park walk. Rosi Braidotti's conception of "nomadic subject" (2014: 170–175) gets reinforced, especially at the very point when Okra needs to collect the remnants of her body from the mouths of bats.

While Plath and Shange's poems, thematically, employ similar and quite usual treatments of female poetic persona at the heart of bare nature, where she has always been thought to originally belong to, their forms resist these accustomed associations, in turn, stereotyping. Indeed, the endings of both poems project their structural resistances embedded in their intertextual dialogues and intergeneric forms. While Plath's poetic persona "foam"'s and "melt"'s at the end of the ride, Okra' body "split"'s at the end of the park walk. Their bodily departures from Ariel and Greens, commonly, reflect on their uneasy encounters with themselves. As the endings echo, the poem's continuous incorporations of fragments and run-ons, two seemingly opposite structures of language, challenge the linguistic sense of sentence formation. As the beginnings and endings get interwoven, with this technique, the notion of cycle becomes more highlighted, and this, in turn, better accommodates a posthumanistic stance at the hearts of Plath and Shange's poems. To support this idea, both poems finish with references to the sunrise, which, indeed, stands for the repetitive cycle of day, as day and night. The sense of "hybridity" gets constantly evoked in the poet's choices of content and form, a Bhabhaian call for "the third space" (1994) locates in their journeys within nature, the moments of peace and self-identification that operates more on collectivistic rather than individualistic realm, reflecting on the female poetic personas' long neglected "nomadic" quests.

References

Bhabha, Homi K. *The Locations of Culture*. New York: Routledge, 1994.

Braidotti, Rosi. "Writing as a Nomadic Subject". *Comparative Critical Studies* II. 2-3 (2014): 163–184.

hooks, bell. *Talking Back: thinking feminist, Thinking black*. Boston: South End P, 1989.

Lester, Neale A. Ntozake Shange: A Critical Study of Her Plays. New York and London: Garland P, 1995.

Plath, Sylvia. "Ariel". *The Collected Poems by Sylvia Plath*, Harper & Row P, 1981.

Pope, Alexander. "An Essay on Criticism".

Shange, Ntozake. From Okra to Greens. St. Paul: Coffee House P, 1984.

"The signifying monkey". www.louisianafolklife.org/lt/articles_essays/creole_art_toast_tradition.html

Hybrid Reading Process as a Strategy for Inclusion: Toni Morrison's *Recitatif* and *Desdemona*

With its suggestion of a dynamic reader within the reading process, reader response theory opens a space for readerly involvement as well as a potential ground for the act of rewriting and in turn offers an inclusive approach towards subjects engaged in the reading process. Incorporating reader response theory and postcolonial approach, Toni Morrison's *Recitatif* and *Desdemona* thematically and structurally celebrate this in-between process as a strategy for inclusion.

Awarded as canonical during her lifetime, the Nobel Prize-winning celebrated writer Toni Morrison stands as a distinguished figure of global literature. One of the key markers of Morrison's distinct style lies in the way she tells stories of a Midwest American background, enabling the story to be heard on both individual and collective levels while providing a bridge between local and global experiences. Toni Morrison is widely known for her striking novels and her challenging nonfiction works, as well as children's books, which she wrote in collaboration with her son Slade Morrison. As for Toni Morrison's works in different genres, they are considerably less known, although Morrison published three stage plays, one poetry collection, as well as one short story published in the Norton Anthology of American Literature. Published in 1985, her only short story, *Recitatif* has not yet received the critical attention it deserves, similar to her 2011 stage play, *Desdemona*, despite the innovative perspective they offer in providing multiple-layered dialogues with the reading process itself.

Since the publication of her celebrated, Pulitzer Prize-winning novel *Beloved* in 1987, the late Toni Morrison has always had a distinguished place in the global literary canon. Morrison is highly acclaimed for her strong narrative techniques surrounding her intriguing stories in her novels the long list of which includes *The Bluest Eye* (1970), *Sula* (1977), *Tar Baby* (1981), *Beloved* (1987), *Jazz* (1992), *Paradise* (1988), *Love* (2003), *A Mercy* (2008), *Home* (2012) and *God Help The Child* (2015). Morrison has also published several children's books, one collection of poems, three drama plays, several works of nonfiction and one short story, which are comparatively less studied despite their inspiring contents and innovative literary methods. The purpose of this study is to examine Morrison's only short story, *Recitatif* (1985), published in Norton Anthology of American Literature, and her latest drama play, *Desdemona* (2011), a postcolonial feminist adaptation of William Shakespeare's *Othello* in the form of a post-sequel. Literature survey displays far more than a satisfactory number of postcolonial, feminist criticism and narratological studies accompanying Toni Morrison's work while there is still limited study on reception studies and inclusivity, two noteworthy qualities of Morrison's work, and Toni Morrison. Looking closely at *Recitatif* and *Desdemona*, this study aims to offer a new insight as well as orientation into Toni Morrison's two less studied works.

Morrison's short story "Recitatif", which opens with Twyla's retrospective narration of her childhood experience in an orphanage called St. Bony's, gradually starts a challenging process for the reader, as soon as Twyla notes that she has to room with Roberta, "a girl from a whole other race" (Morrison 1998: 2079). Reader gets involved in an investigation of unrevealed racial identities of Twyla and Roberta, who together look like "salt" and "pepper" (1998: 2079) as Twyla shares that the older girls in the orphanage use the expression to refer to them. The plot of the text revolves around four encounters of Twyla and Roberta, years after their departure from St. Bony's. The readers witness to the growing class difference between them in each and every encounter. References to Twyla initially as a waitress and later as a fireman's wife and to Roberta initially as Twyla's customer and later as an IBM executive's wife with a limousine mark the gap between their levels of income as well as social status. Their only shared ground is the unpleasant childhood experience in the orphanage where they were being bullied for being left out, in other words, the only children "without beautiful dead parents in the sky" (1998: 2079). In this respect, Twyla and Roberta's tense conversations about what happened to Maggie, the disabled help in the orphanage, act as a mediator for their relations, while Twyla and Roberta's varying memories of Maggie's race reflect on the reader's parallel search for their racial backgrounds.

Although the issue of race seems to be a foregrounding theme at the very beginning, Morrison takes a writerly strategy to not reveal the races of Twyla and Roberta, despite the racist markers introduced initially by Twyla:

> The minute I walked in and the Big Bozo [the director of the orphanage] introduced us, I got sick to my stomach. It was one thing to be taken out of your own bed early in the morning- it was something else to be stuck in a strange place with a girl from a whole other race. And Mary, that's my mother, she was right. Every now and then she would stop dancing long enough to tell me something important and one of the things she said was that they never washed their hair and they smelled funny. Roberta sure did. Smell funny, I mean. [...], (Morrison 1998: 2079).

and subsequently by Roberta's mother, who refuses to shake hands with Twyla's mother:

> Roberta's mother looked down at me and then looked down at Mary too" (1998: 2082).

However, as soon as Maggie gets introduced to the text, the reader senses the presence of alternative reading paths besides the racial context of the short story. Twyla and Roberta's contradictory memories of Maggie and whether they hit her in the orchard are, perhaps, projections of their different conceptions of one another as well as themselves. Scared by the "gar girls", the elder girls bullying them, Twyla and Roberta suppress the incidents in the orchard, which signifies their insecure childhood. The gar girls stand for what they lack, a childhood background similar to the rest of the girls. Given this context, what unites them, not having "beautiful dead parents in the sky" (Morrison 1998: 2079), is stronger than the contrast in their appearances, which makes them be called "salt and pepper" (1998: 2079). In this respect, memories of the kitchen woman Maggie function as a looking-glass through which Twyla and Roberta can view both each other and themselves. Maggie's "sandy colored" (Morrison 1998: 2080) skin is also a strong signifier of unification and separation of the two girls.

Reminiscent of Homi K. Bhabha's conception of "hybridity" as "one and Other while at the same time neither the one nor the Other" (1998: 5), Twyla and Roberta compose the hybrid when joined. On the other hand, a hybrid is the Other of both black and white. This interpretation accounts for a chain of tense arguments between Twyla and Roberta whenever they refer to Maggie and the orchard. Twyla initially notes that she is somehow obsessed with the orchard while "[n]othing really happened there" (Morrison 1998: 2080), to which she later adds "[n]othing all that important" (2080), only Maggie fell down and the elder girls laughed at her. The memory gap is further revealed during the second encounter after St. Bony's, with Roberta's correction of Twyla's memory: "Maggie didn't fall" (1998: 2086); "[…] They knocked her down. Those girls pushed her down and tore her clothes. In the orchard" (1998: 2086).

As Twyla and Roberta meet as parents in a school strife where they support opposite sides, Roberta calls Twyla "[t]he same state kid who kicked a poor old black lady when she was down on the ground" (Morrison 1998: 2089). While Twyla refuses Roberta's accusation by saying "She wasn't black" (1998: 2089), instead of simply saying "I didn't kick her", the delayed revelation of their races highlights. Roberta's following address to Twyla on Christmas Eve foregrounds that race is no more than a single signifier in the comprehensive short story:

> Listen to me. I really did think that she was black. I didn't make that up. I really thought so. But now I can't be sure. I just remember her as old, so old. And because she couldn't talk- well, you know, I thought she was crazy. She'd been brought up in an institution like my mother was and like I thought I would be too. And you were right. We didn't kick her. It was the gar girls. Only them. But well, I wanted to. I really wanted them to hurt her. I said we did it, too. You and me, but that's not true. And I don't want you to carry that around. It was just that I wanted to do it so bad that day- wanting to is doing it (Morrison 1998: 2091).

In reconciliation, the issue of race gets disregarded, and their childhood becomes foregrounded to effectively reinforce Toni Morrison's writerly strategy in choosing not to fix the racial markers and to focus on childhood, the unifying story of the human soul. In the final encounter, Twyla shares that the kitchen woman Maggie, whom Twyla centrally recalls with her "legs like parenthesis" (Morrison 1998: 2080), probably reminded her of Mary, her own dancing mother, with the sound when she is around. In response, Roberta notes that Maggie's muteness possibly reminded her of her own hospitalised mother. In other words, the ongoing argument surrounding Maggie, which reaches its peak during the times of racism, is finally resolved through Maggie. Drawing on these references, race may be taken as an instrument to initiate a free signification process, which, in turn, celebrates the text's potential for reception studies. Toni Morrison's note on "Recitatif" as "an experiment in the removal of all racial codes from a narrative about two characters of different races for whom racial identity is crucial" (1992: xiii), in her theoretical study *Playing in the Dark*, also supports this perspective.

In her article entitled "Black Writing, White Reading and the Politics of Feminist Interpretation", the American critic Elizabeth Abel offers a reader-centred reading of "Recitatif" by foregrounding their different readings of the text with her black colleague, Lula Fragd (Abel 1997: 103). Abel shares that she was sure that Twyla was white, while Lula Fragd was very much convinced that she was black. Trudier Harris, a black American scholar, reflects upon her reading process of "Recitatif" in the following lines: "The cultural/racial stereotypes keep coming at us, and we keep reading, watching, and working hard to uncover the real racial identities" (Abel 1997: 111). The reader of "Recitatif" is predestined to bring into the text all his/her cultural associations. Different reading experiences are also invited by the open-ended parameters of the text itself.

It is noteworthy to address the text's potential for evoking empathy toward, by any means a dissimilar subject by focusing on one common content. Given the context of my six-years-long teaching experience of undergraduate "Postcolonial Literatures in English" classes at İstanbul Bilgi University, I had a chance to closely observe the variety of readerly markers the text enables. One striking observation is that despite the abundance of reading paths about Twyla and Roberta's backgrounds, Maggie was commonly read as a hybrid. A majority of my students who were convinced that Twyla was white, based on the narrations about childhood, noted that the second encounter at the cafe implied the opposite. Similarly, most of the students who at the beginning thought that Roberta was white, preconditioned by the race of the writer, later argued that she was black, drawing on the part where Roberta accused Twyla of "kick[ing] a black lady". Those who had a consistent argument during the three encounters finally accepted that they got confused during the strife at school. As for empathy with any of the characters, a majority of them noted that they felt close to either both or neither. In open-ended discussions, it was noted that it was during the childhood memories of the girls that the majority felt empathy for. As contemporary theories on teaching also demonstrate, collaborative modes of learning, which acknowledge students' individual experiences, contribute to better reception of academic content (Kaplan and Miller 2007: 111). As its title also implies, the structure of "Recitatif" as an open text fits into this criterion. In all these aspects, "Recitatif" provides a valuable tool for an interactive and inclusive classroom environment, which operates through its readers' consistent engagement in a dynamic reading process as well as its reconciliatory approach to the issue of difference by foregrounding common experience for the sake of empathy.

Morrison's 2012 stage play *Desdemona* was initially performed in collaboration with the infamous stage director Peter Sellars and the Malian singer and songwriter Rokia Traore. While the play offers a postsequel to Shakespeare's *Othello*, revisiting the canonical work in a postcolonial feminist context, its major innovation lies in its extended incorporation of the character Barbary, Desdemona's black nanny, into the plot. Given this context, Peter Sellars's note in his Foreword to the play that Shakespeare had also imagined Barbary, although he did not write for her, needs to be highlighted (Sellars 2012: 8). In Act IV Scene III, Desdemona tells her maid Emilia about the story of Barbary and starts singing the Willow's Song, which Barbary taught her:

> My mother had a maid called Barbary.
> She was in love, and he she loved proved mad
> And did forsake her. She had a song of willow,
> An old thing 'twas, but it expressed her fortune,
> And she died singing it. That song tonight
> Will not go from my mind. [I have much to do
> But to go hang my head all at one side
> And sing it like poor Barbary. Prithee, dispatch. (Shakespeare 1988: 1 28-35)

Although Barbary is not a developed character in Shakespeare's play, her song has a significant function in the Shakespearean plot as it foreshadows the approaching tragic ending. Together with Othello's handkerchief, which an Egyptian woman gave his mother and he gave to Desdemona as a family gift, the song can also be taken as a metaphor to connect to the stories of Africa and those of women. While Othello takes the loss of the handkerchief as a sign of Desdemona's betrayal, the handkerchief also implies the failure of female bondage. Emilia, who contributes to Iago's plan, is reminded of empathy with Desdemona singing the Willow's song in emotional connection with an earlier generation African woman's story, to lead to Emilia's sorrowful lament for Desdemona's death in Act V. In other words, the climax that the loss of the handkerchief introduces gets resolved through the willow's song, incorporating individual stories about Africa and of women. In that respect, though not represented as characters, the stories of the two African women, namely the Egyptian woman and Barbary, have significant functions within the Shakespearean plot.

Through Barbary, Morrison also adds to the canonical work the missing story of Desdemona falling in love with Othello. Desdemona feels attraction towards Othello when, invited by her father, Othello tells them intriguing stories about Africa. Incorporating the story of Barbary into the plot, Morrison gives Desdemona an African background, which also accounts for her sudden attachment to Othello through her childhood connection to African folklore through Barbary:

> My solace in those eearly days lay with my nurse, Barbary. She alone encouraged a slit on that curtain. Barbary alone conspired wth me to let my imagination run free. She told me stories of other lives, other countries. Places where gods speak in thundering Silence and mimic human faces and forms. When nature is not a crafted, pretty thing, but wild, sacred and instructive (Morrison 2012: 18).

The above quote is taken from Morrison's *Desdemona* as she shares her young memories about their maid, Barbary, and Barbary's considerable influence in shaping her free-spirited identity. In these aspects, her lines are reminiscent of the lines below where Shakespeare's *Othello*, in Act I, Scene III, tells about Desdemona's attentive response as she listens to him telling his adventurous stories: Wherein I spoke of most disastrous chances:

> Of moving accidents by flood and field,
> Of hairbreadth 'scapes i' th' imminent deadly breach,
> Of being taken by the insolent foe
> And sold to slavery, of my redemption thence,
> And portance in my traveler's history,
> Wherein of antres vast and deserts idle,
> Rough quarries, rocks, (and) hills whose (heads)
> touch heaven,
> It was my hint to speak—such was my process—

And of the cannibals that each (other) eat, The Anthropophagi, and men whose heads
(Do grow) beneath their shoulders. These things to hear
Would Desdemona seriously incline (Shakespeare 1988: 1155–1170).

Morrison's drama play gives Othello another dimension, rereading him through Desdemona's perspective, as a replacement for the dead Barbary. Desdemona's remark that as they danced with Othello, they felt as if they had known one another all their lives (Morrison 2012: 23) reinforces the idea of such a connection. Morrison's play collaborates with Shakespearean tragedy in offering a similar depiction of Africa as an address providing a direct access to nature, while she also offers a critique in revisiting Africa as "wild, sacred and instructive" (Morrison 2012: 18) rather than a place with "cannibals that each other eat" (Shakespeare, 1168). In his Foreword to *Desdemona*, Peter Sellars addresses Shakespeare's *Othello*'s major bias as representing an "imagined Africa", while he introduces Desdemona as a challenge to that aspect (Morrison 2012: 7–11). Morrison's extended engagement with the character "Barbary", a name which means "Africa", also frees the character from being stereotypically received. Called frequently as "Barbary" by Desdemona, she finally announces her real name, "Sa'ran", and asserts that "Barbary" was a name she was given at work. In this respect, Morrison's play reflects on the stereotypical implications of the name "Barbary" as well as its adjective form "Barbarian", which, in their word connotations, signify the stereotyping of Africa and Africans more than "Africa" and "African". As indicated in the lines below, where Desdemona speaks of her, Barbary, as given a life, stands for Desdemona's connection to indigenous sources of African culture, including storytelling, blues and dance:

She was more alive than anyone I knew and more moving. She tended me as though she were my birth mother: braided my hair, dressed me, comforted me when I was ill and danced with me when I recovered (Morrison 2012:18).

The image of a caring subject as accompanied by dancing, singing and story-telling extends to Desdemona's secure childhood memories and reinforces her choice of Othello as husband. Desdemona's earlier note that in their initial encounter, she felt as if she had known Othello all her life (Morrison 2012: 23) also contributes to this idea. In all these aspects, Morrison's *Desdemona* provides readers of *Othello* with a valuable tool as well as new critical dimensions.

An intriguing reader-response strategy was undertaken in "Recitatif", where none of the possible readings of Twyla and Roberta's racial identities can make the story a complete one. Moreover, the parameters of the text also require readers' hybrid-centred focus, embodied metaphorically through the character Maggie. In other words, in order to enable a consistent reading process, the readers are invited to look at both Twyla and Roberta through the hybrid gaze, as signified by the presentation of Maggie as an ultimate destination, as a debatable but still reconciliatory ground of reference. Drawing on the same premises of reader response theory, which suggests:

> Even in the simplest story there is bound to be some kind of blockage, if only for the fact that no tale can ever be told in its entirety. Indeed, it is only through inevitable omissions that a story will gain its dynamism. Thus whenever the flow is interrupted and we are led off in unexpected directions, the opportunity is given to us to bring into play our own faculty for establishing connections-for filling in the gaps left by the text itself (Iser 1980: 216).

Toni Morrison, in *Desdemona*, continues telling the unfinished story of Othello, adding to his story initially told by Cynthio in *Un Capitano Moro* and Shakespeare in *Othello*. Having taught *Desdemona* in my "Adaptations" class, I have observed that the readers of *Desdemona* who are also the readers of *Othello* get more engaged in the representation of Barbary. In our class discussions, most of my students responded positively to the rising question of whether, drawing on her childhood connection to Barbary, we could call Desdemona culturally hybrid. My individual experience in including *Desdemona* in my course syllabus has been remarkably positive, owing to the parameters of the text, which enabled an interactive engagement of its readers, besides the reconciliatory ground for a smooth discussion process. By both its content and structure, Morrison's *Desdemona* reinforces an inclusive learning environment that is usually defined as a secure social area where each and every student feels support and belonging, regardless of their individual qualities and backgrounds (Kaplan and Miller 111). In other words, *Desdemona*'s thematic and structural characteristics enable and support an interactive and inclusive learning environment.

To be more specific, *Desdemona* calls for a hybrid stance in providing a black-centered version of a white-centered story. Adaptation, by nature, stands as an "in-between" process to initiate a dialogue between the source text and the adaptation. This dialogue usually transcends the limits of an authorial dialogue and involves contextual dialogues where cultural texts are inevitably embedded in literary texts and also speaking to one another. The adaptation studies scholar Julie Sanders calls adaptation a "hybrid" (Sanders 2006: 17–19) genre and notes that she draws on Homi K. Bhabha's conception of the term in her own definition. Bhabha's notion of " cultural translation " (Bhabha 2000: 5–7) is also relevant to this discussion as adaptation involves cultural translation, the hybrid quality of which enables smooth dialogues. Homi K. Bhabha's extension of his argument to a metaphorical destination, which he addresses as "the third space", is equally noteworthy, given the context of adaptation, which innately calls for cultural encounters and structurally accommodates possibilities of intercultural dialogues. Borrowing Bhabha's wording, he uses to define "the third space" (2000: 40–43), I wish to address adaptation both as the form and the process where "cultural identities co-exist" and "finally reconcile". In offering Barbary as a central character in her *Desdemona*, Toni Morrison speaks to and speaks through *Othello* by Shakespeare. Adding to *Othello*, with her contemporary consciousness, the story of underrepresented Barbary as Sa'ran, Toni Morrison collaborates with Shakespeare in challenging the limits of his timely context, an attempt previously undertaken by Shakespeare, who had thought about Africa and its then present signifiers, made it even more visible in his text with his choice of an African protagonist, in innovation and courage.

Consequently, two of Toni Morrison's less studied works, her only short story "Recitatif" and her drama play *Desdemona*, a postcolonial feminist rewrite of Shakespeare's *Othello*, need to be foregrounded as two inspiring texts to engage the reader's individualised processes of reading in a targeted dialogue with collectivity. This process in turn evokes possibilities of empathy towards the other as well as reconciliation with the dissimilar. As accommodated within their own generic qualities, both texts by Morrison situate their readers on an in-between axis, standing at the crossroads of multiple encounters between past and present, individual and collective, colonial and postcolonial contemporary and canonical experiences. In doing so, the two texts by Morrison enable intercultural encounters to run smoothly and address their location as "the third space" (Bhabha 2000: 40–43), drawing on Homi K. Bhabha's metaphorical conception of the term. In this respect, Morrison's reader is witness to possibilities of "hybrid" textual formations, calling for hybrid reading processes and invited to experience these intriguing stages of "cultural negotiation" (Bhabha 2000: 5–7) to lead to a final reconciliation. In all these aspects, the incorporation of Morrison's "Recitatif" and *Desdemona* into the literature curriculum provides a smooth ground of discussion and idea exchange by showing possibilities of and highlighting the significance of empathy, both of which in turn reinforce inclusive strategies in the classroom environment.

References

Abel, Elizabeth. "Black Writing, White Reading". *Female Subjects in Black and White*. Ed.

Elizabeth Abel, Barbara Christian and Helene Moglen. Berkeley, Los Angeles and London: University of California Press, 1997.

Barthes, Roland. *S/Z*. Trans. Richard Miller. New York: Hill and Wang: The Noonday P, 1974.

Bhabha, Homi. *The Location of Culture*. London and New York: Routledge, 2000.

Iser, Wofgang. "The Reading Process. A Phenomemonological Approach." *Reader-response Criticism: From Formalism to Poststructuralism*. Ed. Jane P. Tompkins. Baltimore: Johns Hopkins UP, 1980.

Kaplan, M. and A.T. Miller (Eds). "Scholarship of Multicultural Teaching and Learning." *New Directions for Teaching and Learning.* 2007.

Morrison, Toni. *Playing in the Dark*. London: Picador P, 1993.

Morrison, Toni. "Recitatif". *The Norton Anthology of American Literature*. V2. New York and London: Norton &Company, 1998.

Morrison, Toni. *Desdemona*. London: Oberon Books, 2012.

Sanders, Julie. *Adaptation and Appropriation*. London and New York: Routledge, 2006.

Sellars, Peter. "Foreword". *Desdemona*. London: Oberon Books, 2012.

Shakespeare, William. *"Tragedies"*. *The Tragedy of Othello, The Moor of Venice*. London: Marshall Cavendish, 1988.

Index